BEHIND THE FRANCHISE CURTAIN

The Ten Key Elements of Franchising

Richard J. Basch

AUTHORITY
PUBLISHING

Behind the Franchise Curtain: The Ten Key Elements of Franchising

By Richard J. Basch

1. Business & Economics : General 2. Business & Economics : Entrepreneurship 3. Business & Economics : Franchises

ISBN: 978-1-935953-3

Cover design by Lewis Agrell

Cover and author photography courtesy of e2Photography, LLC

Steven Seelig

www.e2photo.net

Printed in the United States of America

Authority Publishing
11230 Gold Express Dr. #310-413
Gold River, CA 95670
800-877-1097
www.AuthorityPublishing.com

Dedication

To my wonderful and amazing children, Nicholas and Samantha, you are my world, my light, and the reason my life is worth living. I love you with all my heart and soul and I'm so very proud of the wonderful people you've become.

And to my mother Natalicia and brother Daniel, you have been my rocks through good times and bad, and I am so fortunate to have such a loving and supporting family—thank you from the bottom of my heart. And finally, to my father, Professor Emeritus Paul F. Basch, Ph.D., who was a prolific author in his own right and is reading over my shoulder from a better place—I'm keeping the family tradition alive, Dad, and I love you.

Can someone get me a hanky? Seriously—this stuff always gets me.

Acknowledgements

This book is the result of more than 15 years of BST (that's blood, sweat, and tears) working in the franchise trenches, much of them in the franchise management and consulting fields, as well as working directly with hundreds of dedicated, salt-of-the-earth franchisees.

I would like to thank the editors, designers, and compositors of Authority Publishing, particularly Stephanie Chandler, president and CEO, and Amberly Finarelli, my editor, for their tireless work on this labor of love.

My sincere gratitude also goes to my many mentors and colleagues, all of whom have had a significant impact on my life, both personally and professionally. In particular, I would like to thank Joe Mathews of the Franchise Performance Group for approving the inclusion of his remarkable K.A.S.H. and "Five Phases of the Franchisee Lifecycle" concepts, both of which have revolutionized the world of franchise consulting. I would also be remiss in not acknowledging the groundbreaking work of Greg Nathan, founder of the Franchise Relationships Institute and author of two seminal works, *The Franchise E-Factor* and *Profitable Partnerships*. I am indebted to Greg as well for approving the inclusion of his "Six Stages of the Franchise E-Factor" content and graphics. Both Joe and Greg have been tireless advocates and supporters of the "franchisee perspective" in franchising, and have opened my eyes to the true meaning of "win-win" franchising.

And finally, to all the passionate and generous individuals at the International Franchise Association who work tirelessly day in and day out to promote the interests of franchisors, franchisees, and small-business owners everywhere—I salute you.

Contents

Author's Note

This book is dedicated to all of the hardworking franchisors and franchisees out there who bust their butts every day to build great franchise systems based on mutual trust and cooperation. Anyone with a few bucks in his or her pocket can buy a franchise or become a franchisor, but it takes a truly unique and compassionate individual to look beyond the money and ask, "How can we ALL win?" Far too many franchisors are entirely preoccupied with their own profitability, while ignoring the profitability of their franchisees. By the same token, far too many franchisees are perfectly willing to blame their lack of success on their franchisors instead of taking a good, hard look in the mirror and accepting responsibility for their actions. Can't we all just get along?

A few words of wisdom from the trenches. For you franchisors (or prospective franchisors) out there, franchisees are *not* employees, nor are they idiots, and most have very little tolerance for B.S. If you're a fat-cat executive-type whose idea of franchising is, "The franchisees take all the risk while I make all the money," you're in for a rude awakening. And for you franchisees (or prospective franchisees), while many franchisors are not greedy SOB's bent on lining their own pockets, some are, so BE AWARE and BE SMART in your decision making. In addition, you should know that if you're the type of person who's unwilling to follow a system because you truly believe that you already know it all, please know that when you fail (and yes, I said *when*), YOU are the problem and YOU are the reason why you didn't make it.

Whew, that was certainly cathartic!

Chapter 1
The Big Picture

DEAR GENTLE READER,

If you've purchased, borrowed, or stolen a copy of this book, you're probably either a franchisor or a franchisee (or a prospective franchisor or franchisee) hoping to make some big bucks in the wonderful world of franchising. Oh sure, you're passionate about the product or service you plan to offer (or are currently offering), and you probably believe you're doing mankind a huge favor by selling more burgers or cleaning more office buildings, but please don't try to B.S. a B.S.'er. At the end of the day you're just trying to make a buck like everyone else (which, by the way, is not a bad thing).

This book is unique for a number of reasons: First, it's written by a guy who's actually been in the trenches as both a franchisee and franchise executive, and who's seen the good, the bad, and the ugly underbelly. Second, it's written from the perspective of both the franchisee and the franchisor, which provides a unique firsthand point of view. Third, it's chock-full of real-world examples and useful behind-the-scenes hints and information. Fourth, it presents an extremely powerful yet user-friendly concept known as the "Ten Key Elements of

Franchising," which, when properly executed, will virtually guarantee untold riches and world domination. OK—perhaps that last statement was a bit on the strong side. Let's just say that when you "go for the green," the Ten Key Elements of Franchising will most likely generate both dollars and significant personal satisfaction. (I'm sure you franchising attorneys out there will appreciate that last bit of personal censorship/CYA on my part.)

If you are a franchisor (or prospective franchisor), I know for a fact that right now you are all atwitter regarding the following concepts:

1) Franchising is a "low-risk" business model wherein the franchisee takes the majority of the risk.

2) You can make good money without having to invest significant capital in a bricks-and-mortar operation.

3) You can create a flock of "golden geese" that will eventually become the greatest annuity ever.

4) And—if you're already a small-business owner—you love the fact that you can grow your empire by leveraging the passion and energy of other entrepreneurs who are just…like…you (you hope).

For you franchisees (or prospective franchisees) out there, *your* brain is preoccupied with champagne wishes and caviar dreams. You're most likely rabidly passionate about dog grooming or the art of sandwich making or the magic of dry cleaning, or whatever floats your boat. You are obsessed with the idea that for the (relatively nominal) cost of a franchisee fee, you will be magically anointed with the "secret formula" that will guarantee your success and deliver you from evil. You believe in your heart of hearts that you are *way* smarter than those other poor saps who tried to start a small business without the loving protection and guidance of a benevolent and all-knowing franchisor. And last but not least, you firmly believe that franchisors always put their franchisees' best interests first, and that their primary reason for existing is to ensure the health, happiness, and well-being of their franchisees.

Well, guess what? I hate to rain on your parade, but like most things in life, it ain't that simple. As a matter of fact, the dirty little secret that many in the franchising community don't want you to know is that operating a franchise (as either a franchisee or a franchisor) is actually *much* harder than it looks, and probably much harder than you ever imagined. Sorry to pee in your Cheerios, but nothing in life that's worth much comes easy, and franchising is certainly no exception.

Now, before you slit your wrists or slink back to your miserable paper-pushing job in that cube farm, please take heart. I wouldn't have written this book or spent the better part of my career in this industry if I believed the concept of franchising was crap—it's not. Not by a long shot. I've personally witnessed many a franchisor and a statistically significant number of franchisees become enormously wealthy and successful by working hard and building great businesses. When executed effectively, the franchise model can be a thing of true beauty.

From a personal standpoint, my primary purpose in writing this book was to get beyond all of the stiff textbook language and touchy-feely stuff out there and write a book that really tells it like it is. I also wanted to share the magic of the Ten Key Elements of Franchising system, because I personally designed and have tested it over many years and by golly, it really works! By now, you've probably come to the conclusion that this is not your grandfather's franchising book—and you are correct. If you're looking for yet another run-of-the-mill, milk-toast, "how-to" book, you need only conduct a quick Google search or take a drive over to your local Barnes and Noble (if they haven't gone the way of Borders Books yet), where you'll find dozens of examples. If, however, you're looking for a no-B.S. look into the world of franchising from a guy who's truly been there and done that (cheesy, I know), you've come to the right place.

So, on to the Ten Commandments...er...Ten Key Elements of Franchising. Wow, talk about delusions of grandeur!

THE TEN KEY ELEMENTS OF FRANCHISING

Like any serious business undertaking, franchising can be both extremely rewarding and painfully challenging, so don't buy into the hype that franchise-based businesses are *much* more likely to be successful than non-franchised businesses. If you have no clue what you're doing, a franchise-based business will kick your butt just as hard as any other small business and in some cases, even harder. That, by the way, is equally true for both franchisors and franchisees. So while we're on the topic, let's discuss the somewhat controversial subject of franchise success/failure rates for a moment. While many articles have been published regarding this topic, cutting through the noise to get to a *real* answer can be frustrating. This is due in large part to what's commonly referred to as the spin factor. The term "spinning" is defined in dictionary.com as, "Noun: *Slang.* A particular viewpoint or bias, especially in the media; slant."[1]

In other words, if you're extremely passionate about your particular point of view, you can always find a way to skew the perspective in your favor. Many franchise salespeople, for example, have become fond of quoting such "statistics" as, "Over 95% of all franchises are still in business after five years." This statement has taken on an almost mythical aura, the origins of which actually date back to a 1987 (and yes, I said *1987*) study by the U.S. Department of Commerce, which presented these statistics. What franchise salespeople *don't* generally mention is that the Department of Commerce actually stopped conducting such studies in 1987. As a matter of fact, this particular statement became so controversial that in May of 2005 the International Franchise Association (the world's oldest and largest nonprofit trade group representing franchising) published a formal letter to its membership base stating:

> It has come to our attention that some IFA-member companies may be providing information about franchising that is long out of date and no longer presents an accurate picture of the sector.
>
> Of particular concern is information claiming that the success rate of franchised establishments is much greater than that of independent small businesses.
>
> Many years ago, the U.S. Department of Commerce conducted studies about franchising which presented such statistics. That information is no longer valid. The agency stopped conducting such studies in 1987.
>
> We strongly urge you to remove any information from your Web site and published materials that make such a claim. The use of such data, in the absence of current research, could mislead prospective franchisees who are attempting to conduct responsible investigations....[2]

To further complicate matters, there is no central repository of franchisor/franchisee information. Although franchisors are required by law to disclose the failure rates of their franchises, they are not required to register this information with any central authority.

So, how the heck are you supposed to determine the success or failure rate of a franchised business versus a non-franchised business? Well, first, you need to stop worrying about the macro-level discussion of franchising versus the traditional small-business model, because in truth, what you're really looking for is a comforting, one-size-fits-all answer that'll help you sleep at night and feel better about your decision. Second, you need to narrow your field of vision to focus on the specific type of business you're interested in operating. Making broad, sweeping generalizations or lumping incongruous businesses together is not going to provide the answers you're seeking. Third, you need to *go do some homework*—or pay someone to do it for you—and really dig into the data.

Following are a few resources that will prove very helpful in this endeavor:

- U.S. Small Business Administration
  - www.sba.gov/

- U.S. Department of Commerce
  - www.commerce.gov

- U.S. Bureau of Labor Statistics
  - www.bls.gov

- International Franchise Association
  - www.franchise.org

- World Franchising Network
  - www.worldfranchising.com

- Opendata/Socrata.com
  - Enter "franchise" in the search box

- The Franchisor You're Considering
  - Talk to them! (More on this in following chapters.)

- The Franchisees Themselves
  - Talk to them! (More on this in following chapters.)

The bottom line is that there are a multitude of reasons why a particular franchise concept—or any small business for that matter—may succeed or fail, and there is no quick and dirty statistic that neatly encapsulates the entire industry. Following are a few of the most common and widely recognized reasons for small-business failure:

- Lack of experience

- Insufficient capital (money)

- Poor location

- Poor inventory management

- Over-investment in fixed assets

- Poor credit arrangement management

- Personal use of business funds

- Unexpected growth

- Competition

- Low sales[3]

If your goal is to find comfort in franchising success rate statistics, then between the internet and your phone, you have all the tools you need. While this answer will probably not suffice for those data-driven franchise-versus-standard-small-business-model pundits out there, I personally believe that arguing over success rate statistics is time that could be better spent building a great business.

Although this book is written from the perspective of both the franchisee and franchisor, for the sake of simplicity it is organized based on the typical franchisor approach to franchising...prayer! All kidding aside, we will be delving into ten specific "elements" that all franchisors and franchisees alike *must* address to be successful. While many franchisees and franchisors do a fair job of executing these Ten Elements, a select few do an outstanding job of executing them. This, as you can imagine, is no easy feat, and explains why only a very small number of franchisors and/or franchisees ever achieve superstardom. Can you say Subway®, anyone? One thing is for sure: Franchisors and franchisees who do *not* do a good job of addressing these Ten Elements will never truly reach their full potential, and may very well end up folding up their tents and going home. Harsh, you say? Yes. Scary? Yes. Happens every day? You betcha. Being a business owner is not for the faint of heart, and in case you haven't noticed, things are not getting any easier out there.

Well, now that you're thoroughly depressed, please go ahead and pop a Xanax and let's keep going. Heck—it always worked for Mom, right?

If I've heard it once, I've heard it a million times: "Man, I thought I was buying a fool-proof, guaranteed system for success. Where do I start and how the $#@% am I supposed to juggle all of these moving parts?" Well, lucky you—you had the brains to pick up a copy of this book! I'm going to share with you a powerful tool I've developed over the years for managing an entire franchise operation—one that works equally well for both franchisees and franchisors. I call it the Ten Key Elements of Franchising, and it looks a little something like this:

The Ten Key Elements of Franchising – Dashboard

Each of the elements represents a critical component of the franchise model that *must* be implemented effectively for a franchisor or franchisee to flourish. Each individual element has three potential color codes—red, yellow, and green—and the goal is to have all of these elements showing green—simultaneously. If you can pull that off, not only are you super-human, you are most likely making piles of money and probably have a really hot significant other. Since operating a really successful franchise is roughly equivalent to juggling five chainsaws while standing on one foot, you can imagine that this is not a simple undertaking. For those of you who still believe that franchising is a get-rich-quick program…I just happen to have a few chainsaws for sale.

THE COLOR CODES

GREEN: A green element is an indicator that you are doing all (or most) of the right things for a given element, and that you're achieving your stated goal. Oh, I forgot to mention that to determine the color code for each element, you must first create a defined goal against which to measure your progress. I've always been a fan of the saying "What gets measured, gets managed," and although it's a bit trite, it's absolutely true nonetheless. When defining a goal for each category, you should always use the S.M.A.R.T goal-setting technique. That is, each goal should be Specific, Measurable, Agreed-upon, Realistic, and Timetable-based. I'm sure that those of you who are familiar with the S.M.A.R.T. concept may have some slightly different verbiage for this acronym, but hey, this is my book and that's my definition. Put simply, if you are achieving your S.M.A.R.T. goals, each of your elements will be green.

YELLOW: A yellow element means that you are most likely on track or on your way to achieving your goal; however, you're not quite there yet. A yellow indicator is simply an alert that you still have some work to do that should not be ignored. In addition, yellow means that you have not encountered an obstacle that is either insurmountable or that appears to be insurmountable. In my experience, while many obstacles may at first blush appear to be insurmountable, they are generally quite mountable...hmmm...that doesn't sound quite right. Let's just say that most challenges can be overcome with the right amount of persistence and gumption.

RED: And finally, good ol' red. A red element means that you need to be working for someone else (snort, chuckle). OK, really, a red indicator means that something is *way* off relative to your stated goal, and that you'd better pay attention quickly before that something bites you in the butt. Red means "high priority," so blowing off a red element will generally result in pain either financially, operationally, personally, professionally, or all of the above. Just so you know, ignoring red elements and hoping they go away is *not* a viable solution; however, you'd be amazed at how many franchisors and franchisees actually select this "option." Perhaps this is the reason the world is filled with mediocre franchise systems and franchisees, and why at some franchise conferences franchising attorneys outnumber attendees by a ratio of two to one. OK, perhaps that's a bit of an exaggeration but trust me, there is no shortage of franchise attorneys in the world. (More on this in later chapters.)

One of my favorite sayings is, "Go for the green," which I personally feel is brilliant based on the double meaning (get it—green like the franchising element and green like the dollar?). Yes, I am well aware that this little ditty has been around for about a thousand years, but just let me have this one.

When you first become a franchisor or franchisee, all of your elements will most likely be red. Don't panic. It's not that I'm a pessimist (I'm actually quite the optimist); it's just that you probably haven't done much of anything yet, so how could you possibly have achieved your S.M.A.R.T. goals? Now, if you're anything like me (a workaholic perfectionist), you will probably be seized by an uncontrollable urge to hurl every time you look at a dashboard full of red elements, and you'll want to do anything and everything to "go green" ASAP. Don't fight this urge—this is a good thing and I applaud you for being an overachiever with a sensitive stomach. If, on the other hand, you're the type who's perfectly comfortable living in a sea of red, then I'd recommend you immediately withdraw $200,000 in crisp $20 bills, light them on fire, and have yourself a nice little weenie roast. At least you'll stay warm and toasty for a while.

As you begin your franchising journey, some of your Key Elements will be green, some will be yellow, and yes, some will be red. If you think about it, that's really the definition of life, isn't it? How profound...I smell a self-help book in my future!

Listen, just focus on "going for the green" and before you know it, you'll have plenty of real green in your life. Figure 1 indicates how the Ten Key Elements look in the "dashboard" format.

The dashboard is an at-a-glance representation of the overall "health" of your franchise location (or franchise system for you franchisors). Once you've established a S.M.A.R.T. goal for each the Ten Key Elements of Franchising, you will then select a corresponding color for each specific element based on your progress toward your goal (you may want to refer back to the definitions of green, yellow, and red in this chapter). I'm sure there is some amazing algorithm out there that could automatically determine the color of each element based on your stated S.M.A.R.T. goal(s); however, I've found that it's best just to use your own good judgment. Yes, I realize that this is a bit subjective, but by selecting the color code yourself, you'll be forced to think about *why* you're selecting that particular color code, and that's what this system is really all about! Your ultimate goal is to light up your dashboard like a Christmas wreath—nice and green.

In the center of the dashboard listed in Figure 1, you will notice a list of three priorities. Any red elements should be listed as "top priorities" in this "priority" section, followed by the yellow elements (if you have fewer than three red elements). The priority of the elements will again be determined manually based on a holistic view of all of the elements. If you're wondering why Figure 1 only displays three priority items in the center "priority" section, it's because I've found that one can only really focus on three priority items at any time. Trying to focus on more than three priority items is generally an exercise in futility, and will result in too much work, too much stress, and few, if any, quality results. I'm reminded of another old saying that goes, "How do you eat an elephant? Why, one bite at a time, of course." Now that we're aligned on the elements and color codes, let's take a look at each of the Ten Key Elements of Franchising in detail.

CHAPTER NOTES

CHAPTER I: THE BIG PICTURE

1) Dictionary.com Unabridged. Based on the Random House Dictionary, © Random House, Inc. 2012. http://dictionary.reference.com/browse/spinning

2) Posted Thu, 2008/11/06 – 11:26 by Don Sniegowski, BlueMauMau.org, © 2011 by each individual author. All Rights Reserved. http://www.bluemaumau.org/6327/ifa_urges_franchisors_stop_bogus_industry_claims

3) U.S. Small Business Administration. *What are the major reasons for small-business failure?* http://www.sba.gov/content/what-are-major-reasons-small-business-failure

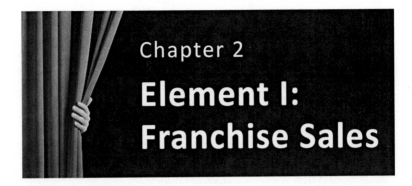

Chapter 2

Element I:
Franchise Sales

Every franchisor, big or small, has a franchise development department. In some cases it is a department of one that may be manned by a passionate (and quite frequently strange and eccentric) founder. In other cases, it may be a massive "bullpen" of franchise salespeople whose entire function in life is to sell, sell, sell—which, by the way, is common in larger franchising organizations. Regardless of the size of the franchisor, the franchise development department exists for one purpose: to sell franchises.

Franchise salespeople are often among the friendliest and most fun-loving people you'll ever meet. With a smile in their voice and a twinkle in their eye, they will quickly and easily make you feel like the smart, sexy, savvy businessperson you know you are, and before you know it you'll be singing their praises from the rooftops. While I'm certainly not implying that there is anything wrong with this process, make no mistake: Franchise development people love you because you represent a big, fat commission check and because they're under tremendous pressure to sell—particularly in the case of a new franchise concept or offering.

Generally speaking, more mature franchisors will employ a vice president of franchise development or even a *senior* vice president of franchise development, whose primary responsibility is to manage the strategic and tactical elements of the franchise sales process. The VPFD's, as they are commonly known, will typically spend the majority of their time studying demographic and psychographic data in an effort to pinpoint the areas of the country that are likely going to be the most receptive to the specific concept or offering. They will pore over maps and charts to plot out various target areas, and they will work closely with the marketing department to create the related marketing collateral to execute their strategy. They will also spend a great deal of time analyzing their "sales pipeline" to determine exactly where their leads are coming from and the return on investment (ROI) for each lead source. A good VPFD will also spend a good chunk of his or her waking hours attempting to forecast future sales performance. This, by the way, is frequently a thankless task that is made even more difficult by the relentless hounding of the senior leadership team and/or president/CEO, who are rarely satisfied with the sales performance. More often than not, the VPFD will be directly responsible for sharing strategy, tactics, and results with a "board of directors" (i.e., a group of wealthy people), so believe me when I say they have *plenty* of motivation to sell, sell, sell. They are also frequently paid quite handsomely, and can easily command a six-figure base salary with a commission structure that can sometimes double or, in select cases, even triple their base compensation. A good VPFD will drive a nice car and live in a beautiful house, but he or she also generally subsists on a diet of coffee and Tums.

Frequently, a franchise development department will also include a director of franchise development and a few "development associates" (or something along those lines), whose job it is to do the actual selling and managing of the tactics so the primary strategy can be executed. These are all generally happy, smiley, affable people who will make you feel good about yourself. Just tell me I'm smart and handsome/beautiful and I'm all yours, right?

The franchise development process is frequently described in the franchising world as a "funnel" (see Figure 2) and is generally broken down into several primary components:

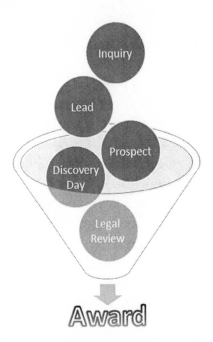

Figure 2: Typical Franchise Development Sales Funnel

1) **THE INQUIRY:** This is usually a brief phone call with a junior franchise development associate responding to an initial inquiry submitted via a website, email, or phone. If you, as the prospective franchisee, don't have any money or if your occupation/skill sets are nowhere near what the franchisor is looking for, you probably won't make it past this step.

2) **THE LEAD:** If you make it past step one, you will be asked to provide some more detailed information regarding your background, income, net worth, etc. This is often referred to as the "candidate qualification," or CQ, phase. If you talked a good game in step one, but in reality you're full of crap and don't have two nickels to rub together, this is probably the end of the line for you.

3) **THE PROSPECT:** If you do, in fact, have a few bucks (or know where to come up with some) and can string a few coherent sentences together, congrats, you've just graduated from lead to prospect. Add to the mix a little relevant business and/or life experience and you're on your way to the webinar.

4) **THE WEBINAR:** This is generally the stage where the franchisor will trot out his or her *oh*-so-compelling and professionally crafted PowerPoint presentation to "wow" you with cool photos, videos, ultra positive testimonials, and generally super happy franchisees. There is nothing inherently wrong with this process and as a matter of fact, I've personally participated in and created many a franchise development webinar myself; however, you need to take it for what it is: an "infomercial" designed to whet your appetite and reinforce your brilliant decision to pursue your dream of owning your very own franchise business.

5) **DISCOVERY DAY:** Assuming you were sufficiently dazzled by the PowerPoint-based webinar and you survived the subsequent follow-up calls, it's time for the "big show"… Discovery Day, or as it's commonly known in franchise lingo, D-Day. D-Day is an opportunity to spend some quality time schmoozing with various members of the executive team (and their minions), and to learn more about what makes their organization so incredibly awesome. It's also the first time you get to meet your future wives/husbands…er business partners. (A franchise really is like a marriage in so many ways. More to come on this in future chapters.)

A NOTE FOR FRANCHISEES

D-Day presents the perfect opportunity to ask the tough questions and to really see the franchisor's team in action, so COME PREPARED WITH PLENTY OF QUESTIONS! If you're meeting with a quality franchisor, please keep in mind that *the franchisor* will be evaluating *you* while you're evaluating the franchisor, so it's always best to bring your A-game. Treat this opportunity as you would a job interview or an important business meeting.

By the time D-Day is over, you should have so many thoughts going through your head that you'll feel like it's going to explode. Don't worry—this is a good thing. Whatever you do, don't assume that your window of opportunity for asking questions is closed once you get back home—it isn't. Write down any and all additional questions and set up some time for a follow-up conversation with your franchise development rep. Remember: Buying a franchise is one of the biggest investments you'll ever make, and you have every right to ask all the questions you want. Go ahead—bug the heck out of your friendly franchise development rep...I'll bet he or she will keep smiling no matter how many times you call. That is, of course, unless you tell him or her you want out.

A word of advice regarding financial questions. If you are working with a franchisor who has chosen not to include a "financial performance representation" (FPR) in Item 19 of the franchise disclosure document (FDD), there is a high probability that you will get seriously pissed off when you can't seem to get a straight answer regarding unit-level economics (gross revenue, profits, cost of goods sold as a percentage of sales, net income, etc.). Although a relatively small percentage of franchisors have made the decision to include FPR's in their FDD's, the majority have not.

Please note that a reluctance on the part of a franchisor to share performance data does not *necessarily* mean that the franchisor has something to hide or that the franchisor's model doesn't work. In reality, it has more to do with the fact that franchisors must be very careful about the claims they make with regard to franchisee performance. In the not too distant past, it was not uncommon for franchise development people to make comments such as, "Unfortunately, I am prohibited by law from providing any financial information"; however, this has since changed based on the amended Federal Trade Commission (FTC) Franchise Rule, which was approved on January 22, 2007 and became mandatory on July 1, 2008. In a nutshell, the FTC now specifically requires franchisors to state in Item 19 of the FDD that they *can* provide financial information, but have chosen not to. The specific language can be found later on in this chapter in the detailed description of the 23 mandated Items included in the FDD.

When I went through this process as a franchise candidate myself, I distinctly remember thinking, "Man, if I could just get my hands on a friggin' profit and loss [P&L] statement or some basic numbers, I could figure out if I can make any money!" Don't fret—all is not lost. By reviewing each of the 23 items in the FDD carefully, you can piece together a fairly accurate framework of your basic expenses. In addition, by making a number of follow-up calls to existing franchisees, you should be able to fill in any blanks. You see, *franchisees* aren't prohibited from sharing detailed financial information because they're considered to be unbiased parties. Here's the real secret: Make those due diligence calls! There simply is no substitute for contacting a broad cross-section of existing franchisees and asking the tough questions, so DO NOT skip this step. You'll also want to pay close attention to Item 7 in the FDD, which details the costs of getting into the business, aka the initial investment. Do all of these things correctly and *voila*—you'll have a nice, reasonably accurate pro forma!

A WARNING FOR FRANCHISEES

Some franchisors may attempt to steer you toward certain specific franchisees who have been pre-selected because they've agreed to share a positive story or because they have been particularly successful. While you can (and should) call a few of these individuals, do not hesitate to call a bunch of other franchisees who aren't on the franchisor's "happy list." You just may hear a very different story. By the way, franchisors are prohibited by law from bribing or inducing franchisees to provide positive validation and also from steering prospects to only the "good" franchisees, so just store this little tidbit in your memory banks for future reference. Take a look at the list of franchisees in Item 20 of the FDD. Since franchisors are required to include contact information for every franchisee, you can randomly select a franchisee and give them a call. The Item 20 information should be listed by city and state if you are interested in the performance of franchised units in a particular geographic area.

A DOUBLE WARNING FOR FRANCHISEES

Beware of *any* franchisor who provides performance guarantees beyond those specifically detailed in the FDD. This is a *ginormous* red flag, and unless you meet certain specific criteria,[4] this is not only unethical, it is illegal.

6) **THE BEHAVIORAL SURVEY:** Although only a relatively small percentage of franchisors have adopted the behavioral or "personality" survey as a standard component of their franchisee selection process, the number is steadily growing. This is a valid and legitimate tool that should provide some comfort to you that the franchisor you're considering is attempting to ensure a good fit for both parties.

There are many types of surveys out there and most of them are quite good, so if and/or when you're presented with a survey, just answer the questions as accurately and honestly as possible and be aware that the franchisor will be comparing your profile against a standard profile he or she's created based on his or her definition of the "optimal" franchisee. Oh, and don't worry—these are not pass or fail "tests," so *always answer as truthfully and honestly as possible.* Personally, I've had some very good experiences with Bill Wagner of Accord Management Systems. Bill is a well-respected speaker and the author of the book *The Entrepreneur Next Door*, and he's been a fixture in the franchising world for many, many years. In my humble opinion, his McQuaig Behavioral Assessment System is among the best in the industry.[5]

It's important to note that while your behavioral survey results may not necessarily knock you out of contention (unless you're a sociopath, kleptomaniac, etc.), they may cause the franchisor to require that you bring on a partner or perhaps hire some key staff members to counterbalance your personality and "round out" the team.

7) **THE LEGAL REVIEW:** This is generally an internal process wherein the legal department (also known by the franchise development department as the "sales prevention department"—yuk, yuk) or in some cases the finance and/or executive team, will look for any final red flags before giving their thumbs up. Remember: Franchise development people are paid a handsome commission every time a new franchisee comes on board, so by the time a prospect makes it to the legal stage, the sales guys and gals are generally biting their nails and praying that you don't have any skeletons in your closet. If you do have a few skeletons, it's best to own up to them early, as this could really haunt you down the road if you don't make it as a franchisee. When in doubt, disclose.

8) **THE AWARD:** Hallelujah, praise…whomever you praise: You made it! You've run the franchisor's gauntlet and he or she has deemed you worthy to go forth and prosper using his or her super cool product and/or service. Whoop, whoop, and all that. Now the *real* fun begins!

FOLLOWING ARE A FEW ADDITIONAL IMPORTANT FRANCHISE DEVELOPMENT PEARLS OF WISDOM FOR YOUR READING ENJOYMENT

MULTI-UNIT OR AREA DEVELOPMENT AGREEMENTS: A multi-unit or area development agreement generally allows a franchisee the right to develop and operate more than one franchise unit in a defined geographic area. As a rule, many franchisors will limit the number of units a franchisee can open (typically 2 to 5), however some may allow a franchisee to open additional locations. The agreement will specify a time frame in which you will need to open each unit, and you will generally lose your exclusive development rights if you do not meet the development schedule requirements.

MASTER FRANCHISE AGREEMENTS: Master franchise agreements provide the master franchisee (either an individual or a corporation), the right to sub-franchise a franchisor's concept within a specific territory, region, state, or even an entire country. In this arrangement, the master franchisor, in many respects, becomes a mini-version of the franchisor. Frequently, master franchisors are responsible for providing ongoing support to their franchisees, such as operations and training, and may also be required to open a specified number of locations (including company-owned units), based on a specific timeframe. As franchisees purchase franchise units from the master franchisor, the franchisor often receives a piece of the action in the form of a percentage of the franchise fee.

THE FRANCHISE DISCLOSURE DOCUMENT (FDD)

The FDD is a document mandated by the FTC for all franchise entities. It is comprised of 23 individual "Items," each with its own specific purpose. Let's take a closer look at each:

ITEM 1: The Franchisor, Its Predecessors, and Affiliates – Requires the disclosure of general background information regarding the franchisor, its parent company, its predecessor companies, and any affiliates that provide goods or services to its franchisees or that offer other types of franchises. This disclosure will identify the franchisor's experience in this type of business and will provide a description of the franchise offered, as well as the market for the goods and/or services provided and the competition that it faces.

ITEM 2: Business Experience – Provides some personal information regarding the officers and directors of the franchising company based on a five-year look-back period. It generally identifies all key personnel and affiliates that play any significant role in the operation of the business.

ITEM 3: Litigation – Provides details pertaining to the history of civil cases related to franchise regulatory and disclosure violations, fraud, unfair or deceptive practices, antitrust, securities laws and other cases that are material to the franchisor, as well as criminal and administrative litigation matters involving the franchisor, its predecessors, parent company and certain of its affiliates, as well as litigation matters related to any of the franchisor's officers, owners, directors, or executives.

ITEM 4: Bankruptcy – Must disclose any bankruptcy in the last 10 years that involved the franchisor, its affiliates, its predecessor, officers, general partners and any of the individuals listed in Item 2 who manage the franchise company.

ITEM 5: Initial Franchise Fees – Is intended to provide a franchisee with an understanding of the fees the franchisee will have to pay to the franchisor or its affiliates (for himself or herself or for a third party) before the franchisee can open his or her business to the public. This item discloses what, if any, refund is available should the agreement not be fulfilled, but it does not disclose any pre-opening fees that must be paid directly to other third parties, as those fees are covered in Items 6 and 7.

ITEM 6: Other Fees – Discloses all fees and payments that must be paid in addition to the upfront money, including service fees, ongoing royalties, renewal fees, training fees, advertising fees, and any other one-time or ongoing charges payable to the franchisor or its affiliates.

ITEM 7: Initial Investment – Provides an estimate of the funds that will be needed to develop the franchise through its opening to the public, and for a reasonable time thereafter (extending at least three months post-opening). A franchisee can expect to invest in equipment, supplies, real estate, furnishings, technology, insurance, construction, working capital, and other costs associated with starting up the business.

ITEM 8: Restrictions and Obligations on Products and Services – Describes the restrictions the franchisor will place on the franchisee with regard to the purchase of products and services used in the franchise. These restrictions encompass three general areas: items that can only be purchased from the franchisor or its affiliates, items that may be purchased only from certain designated suppliers, and items that may be purchased from any suppliers as long as the item meets the franchisor's specification.

ITEM 9: Franchisee's Obligations – Includes a table listing the franchisee's principle obligations, which details the primary areas of responsibility in the business (such as obligations relating to finding and securing real estate). In addition, it provides references to specific sections of both the FDD and the actual franchise agreement that define the legal obligations a franchisee is assuming. This section makes it easy for you to find certain key elements of the legal agreements.

ITEM 10: Financing – Provides information regarding any financing programs, including leases and installment contracts the franchisor may directly or indirectly extend to franchisees.

ITEM 11: Franchisor's Assistance, Advertising, Computer Systems, and Training (Formerly known as Franchisor's Obligations) – Describes the obligations the franchisor has to the franchisee, both pre- and post-opening. It provides details regarding operational assistance, such as marketing/advertising, training, market research, and computer programs provided by the franchisor.

ITEM 12: Territory – Provides details regarding how the territory is established (e.g., by square mileage, population, etc.), and discloses whether the franchisor will grant the franchisee an exclusive or protected territory. The franchisor also must disclose whether it sells the products or services through alternative distribution channels, such as through the internet.

ITEM 13: Trademarks – Provides information regarding the franchisor's principal trademarks, logos, trade names, and commercial symbols registered with the U.S. Patent and Trademark Office.

ITEM 14: Patents, Copyrights, and Proprietary Information – Details the copyrights and patents owned by the franchisor, and may also describe "business trade secrets."

ITEM 15: Participation Obligation – Requires disclosure as to whether the franchisee is obligated to operate the franchised business himself or herself, or whether absentee ownership is permitted.

ITEM 16: Restrictions on What the Franchisee May Sell – Imposes limits and restrictions on what the franchisee may sell. The franchisor also must disclose the extent to which it is permitted to change these requirements.

ITEM 17: Renewal, Termination, Transfer, and Dispute Resolution – Dictates the length of time for which a franchisee will receive a return on his or her investment. This section details all contingencies and options for renewing, terminating, or transferring the business, as well as any mediation procedures for settling disagreements between the franchisor and franchisee. This is another great chart that will enable you to understand the key terms of the legal agreements.

ITEM 18: Public Figures – Requires the franchisor to disclose whether it uses any public figure (famous person) to endorse the franchise. If so, the franchisor is required to disclose the compensation paid or promised to the public figure, the individual's involvement in the management or control of the franchisor, and the amount of the individual's investment in the franchisor.

ITEM 19: Financial Performance Representations (Formerly Known as Earnings Claims) – Provides the actual, average, projected, or forecasted financial sales profits or earnings for the franchisor. Some franchisors do not furnish earnings estimates or projections, and in cases where no financial performance representations are made, the following statement is included: "This franchisor does not make any representations about a franchisee's future financial performance of a company-owned or franchised outlet. We also do not authorize our employees or representatives to make such representations either orally or in writing. If you are purchasing an existing outlet, however, we may provide you with the actual records of that outlet. If you receive any other financial performance information or projections of your future income, you should report it to the franchisor's management by contacting the Federal Trade Commission and appropriate state regulatory agencies."

ITEM 20: Outlets – Lists all of the franchisor's company-owned units currently in operation, and provides details regarding unit openings, closings, transfers and franchise terminations during the previous three years. It also provides the names, telephone numbers, and locations of existing franchisees as well as the contact information for franchisees that have recently left the system.

ITEM 21: Financial Statements – Requires an exhibit that contains the franchisor's audited financial statements for the past three fiscal years, on a comparative basis.

ITEM 22: Contracts – Requires the franchisor to attach to the FDD a copy of all form contracts the franchisee will sign, including the franchise agreement, options, leases, and purchase agreements.

ITEM 23: Receipt – Is the final section and acknowledges receipt of the FDD by the prospective franchisee, but does not obligate the franchisee to sign the agreement.

Keep in mind that fourteen states (as of this printing) add additional disclosure requirements for franchisors who plan to sell franchises in their states. The states of California, Hawaii, Illinois, Indiana, Maryland, Michigan, Minnesota, New York, North Dakota, South Dakota, Rhode Island, Virginia, Washington and Wisconsin require franchisors to include additional disclosures by way of addenda to the FDD that are specific to that state's regulations. Therefore, it is important to review these state-specific addenda in addition to the 23 Items described above.

Generally, in large, well-known franchising organizations the terms of the franchise agreement are non-negotiable—particularly those terms that are of material interest to the organization. In the case of smaller, startup franchising concepts, the franchisor may be more amenable to negotiating aspects of the agreement.

A DOUBLE WARNING FOR FRANCHISEES

Do NOT, under any circumstance, attempt to breeze through the 23 FDD items without the assistance of a competent and experienced franchise attorney. An investment in competent counsel may very well save you hundreds of thousands of dollars, and it is imperative that as a franchisee you understand all of the terms and conditions in the FDD and franchise agreement.

THE BAD FRANCHISOR PERSPECTIVE

"It's going to cost *how much* to create this FDD thing?! Man, I'm in the wrong business! So how long is this going to take? What? I must have misheard you—did you say a month? That's waaaay too long. You don't understand—I have a candidate with cash in hand who's ready to buy this thing today! And do I *really* need to review *every* section, or can you just slap something together and I'll skim through it? Oh, and I hate lawyers, so if we can just skip the legal review that would save me a bundle of dough." You laugh, but I've actually heard this statement uttered almost word-for-word a number of times by various franchisors. Scary…isn't it?

A WARNING

A franchisor who does not respect the FDD is a franchisor who just doesn't get it, and is either just "dabbling" in franchising, or worse, is flying by the seat of his or her pants. Either way, can you say *giant* red flag?

THE BAD FRANCHISEE PERSPECTIVE

"I hate paperwork—it's just such a pain! These guys have come up with an awesome concept and they've all been *so* nice to me…what could possibly go wrong? Besides, my cousin Vinny is a divorce lawyer and he said he'd take a look at this FDD thingy for me. Can't I just sign it and get it over with?" Yes, I've actually heard this perspective as well—seriously.

A WORD TO THE WISE FOR FRANCHISEES

The FDD is one of the most important documents you will ever review, and is easily up there with the purchase of a home or the drafting of a prenuptial agreement (snicker). Unless you're the type of thrill-seeking personality who gets excited by the prospect of gambling huge sums of money, do yourself a favor and spend a few hours of your life getting cozy with the FDD. Leave the gambling for Vegas.

By the way, the franchise agreement, which accompanies the FDD and provides further clarification, is equally as important, so break out a highlighter and review it cover-to-cover as well.

ANOTHER WARNING FOR FRANCHISEES

If a franchise development person ever says something along the lines of, "The FDD is a great replacement for Ambien," or the always popular "Trust me. Do you really think we'd have all of these great franchisees if this concept didn't work?" don't walk—*run* to the restroom, splash some cold water on your face, and repeat out loud, "Snap out of it—they have me under their spell!" Trust me: You'll be in a much better position to see through the hype and analyze the true merits of the product offering. In other words, don't be a chump—read the material!

THE FRANCHISE AGREEMENT

The franchise agreement is included as an exhibit of the FDD so that you will have the opportunity to fully review the agreement before you sign on the dotted line. In a nutshell, the FDD spells out all the responsibilities and expectations for the franchisee and franchisor, and summarizes the terms of the franchise agreement that are important for you to understand and review. If you choose to purchase a franchise, you will sign the franchise agreement, which is the legally binding contract that requires each party to uphold and honor all of the provisions in the franchise agreement, as well as any negotiated items described in any attached amendments or addenda to the franchise agreement.

Every franchise agreement provides certain basic provisions and conditions. These may be placed in different locations, numbered differently, or even have different subtitles, but they are all essentially the same in nature. Although the FDD (summary of the agreement) describes the relationship between the franchisor and franchisee, the franchise agreement (written contract) governs the relationship. In general, if there is a difference between the language in the FDD and the way the franchise agreement reads, the language in the franchise agreement will prevail.

SOME INTERESTING NOTES REGARDING "FRANCHISE SALES OUTSOURCING"

A NOTE FOR FRANCHISORS

One relatively recent trend is the emergence of third-party franchise development organizations, also known in franchise parlance as "franchise sales outsourcing" organizations (FSO's). The popularity of FSO's has grown significantly in the past few years, as many franchisors have come to the conclusion that they simply do not have the skills, resources, or time to develop and cultivate an in-house franchise development department. The FSO concept is also particularly popular with new franchisors who are looking to get off to a quick start, and may not be able to afford to hire a high-powered franchising expert. One of the largest and most successful FSO's, Franchise Dynamics (www.franchisedynamics.net), actually lists on their website the ten reasons why they believe franchise outsourcing works:

1. Minimize your initial investment in franchise sales staff, facilities, and technology

2. Access to top-quality representation that you cannot afford or match with internal staff

3. Improved lead-generation handling and more effective sales activity

4. Daily franchise sales management tasks eliminated

5. More accurate forecasting

6. Eliminate non-buyers earlier in the process, resulting in a shorter selling cycle—more deals, faster

7. More effective selling with higher sale averages from your lead flow—stretching your marketing dollars further

8. Creates stronger franchisee base and improves company image

9. Paying for performance reduces risk

10. Better results, higher growth, at a lower cost per sale[6]

As discussed earlier in this chapter, top franchise sales executives can easily command six-figure salaries, and when factoring in commissions, benefits, training, compliance, and general administrative overhead, developing a franchise sales department is not a chump-change endeavor by any means. That being said, engaging a high-caliber FSO is not exactly an inexpensive venture either, so if you're a franchisor I *strongly* recommend that you put pen to paper and really give some thought to a few key factors, such as how quickly you intend to ramp up, and how much capital you have available to invest in your franchise development efforts.

A NOTE FOR FRANCHISEES

For you franchisees (or prospective franchisees) out there, working with an FSO can often be a positive experience in that for the most part, you'll be working with seasoned pros who typically have many years of experience selling multiple concepts. The largest and most successful FSO's can represent upward of 100 different brands, and as a result, they've become adept at answering just about any question imaginable. On the flip side, however, most FSO's exist for one reason and one reason alone: to sell you a franchise.

FSO's derive the bulk of their revenue from the commissions they earn on a franchise sale, so if you're a "tire kicker" or you just want to pick the brain of a sales guy, don't be surprised if your initial conversation is short and sweet. For those of you who have actually taken the franchise plunge, just be aware that once the ink is dry on your franchise agreement, and your new franchisor has confirmed that your franchise fee has been paid, your former "best franchising buddy" will waste no time in wishing you all the best as he or she sprints for the door. Although the majority of salespeople working for quality FSO's really do care about their franchise candidates and genuinely want them to succeed, once they've sealed the deal, they firmly believe that it's the franchisor's responsibility to ensure that the other nine key elements of franchising are effectively executed.

CHAPTER NOTES

CHAPTER 2: ELEMENT I

4) Sophisticated Investors - The FTC has identified three categories of sophisticated investor transactions in which a franchisor need not provide a disclosure document under the New Rule. These transactions include sales: (1) requiring a large investment ($1 million, excluding unimproved land and money obtained through the franchisor); (2) to experienced franchisees who have been in business for more than 5 years and who have a net worth in excess of $5 million; and (3) to owners and officers of the franchisor. Federal Trade Commission Amended Franchise Rule, 16 C.F.R. § 436.8 (2007)

5) Accord Management Systems, Inc. 1459 E. Thousand Oaks Blvd., Building G, Thousand Oaks, CA 91362 Telephone:1-805-230-2100, Fax:1-805-230-2186, Email: info@accordsyst.com, www.accordsyst.com

6) Franchise Dynamics, LLC © 2011 http://franchise-dynamics.net/whyuseanfso.html

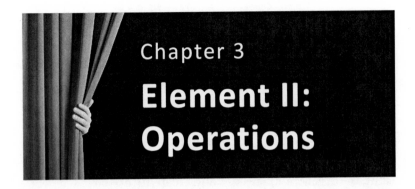

Chapter 3
Element II: Operations

Once you're on board as a full-fledged franchisee and the "courting process" has concluded, it's time to meet your real spouse...er...franchisor. As mentioned earlier, franchising is, in many ways, like a marriage, so you can expect some good times and some not so good times—in sickness and in health, 'til franchising attorneys do us part. (Grin.)

THE FRANCHISE BUSINESS CONSULTANT

TIER 1: The Pre-Opening Business Consultant (POBC)

One of the first people you'll meet when initially coming on board as a new franchisee will most likely be a rather chipper operations individual who will introduce himself or herself as your "pre-opening business consultant" (POBC), or "on-boarder," or something along those lines. This individual is generally responsible for ensuring a smooth pre-opening process and will frequently serve as your single point of contact or SPOC with the franchisor until you officially open your doors for business.

The pre-opening process is a unique time in the franchise lifecycle for both franchisees and franchisors, and most franchisees are basically clueless babes in the woods at this stage in the game. Add to this the fact that many pre-opening processes are one-time-only activities that will not be replicated (such as the first store build-out or the first review of the operations manual), and you have what amounts to a very steep learning curve. This means that the POBC must have the patience of a saint, the organizational skills and creativity of Martha Stewart, and the backbone of Donald Trump. Needless to say, this role is best accomplished by an empathetic, even-tempered type of individual who is comfortable answering really lame questions over and over and over again. If you've ever watched the movie *Groundhog Day*, you'll understand the life of a POBC.

In addition, The POBC is also responsible for adhering to a strict opening timeline, which can often include hundreds of individual action items and encompass every department from operations to accounting. POBC's are not only good at working with new franchisees; they are also adept at bridging the gap between departments, as they need to be chummy with everyone to get things accomplished.

A NOTE FOR FRANCHISEES

Although strong POBC's can be a very important asset, they are generally under *significant* pressure to keep things moving along, so don't be surprised if you occasionally feel like you're being given a good, swift kick in the butt—you are. Believe it or not, franchisors don't make much, or in some cases, *any* money from the initial franchise fee you paid. Those dollars are quickly gobbled up by marketing and administrative costs (aka the "acquisition costs") necessary to bring new franchisees on board. Who do you think pays for all of those happy, shiny franchise development reps? Keep in mind that while a strong new-store sales forecast is important for franchisors, a strong *unit*-opening forecast is just as important if not more so, as this will determine how quickly the royalty dollars will begin to flow in. Although most franchisees tend to focus on the initial franchise fee they've paid, franchisors know that the real magic (read: MONEY) in franchising is the royalty stream created by having multiple franchisees paying a weekly or monthly royalty (aka "ongoing franchise fee"). The quicker the franchisor can get you open, the quicker he or she can get to the big money. To be fair, all franchisees have a vested interest in opening quickly as well for the very same reason (to get paid), so expect a full-court press the moment the ink is dry on the franchise agreement.

A WARNING FOR FRANCHISEES

Some franchisors may include a monetary penalty in their FDD and/or franchise agreement for not opening in a timely manner, so you may want to re-read Item 11 of your FDD to be on the safe side. Franchisors will generally provide an extension if any unanticipated challenges are encountered, such as weather-related issues or zoning changes; however, most franchisors will not be very supportive of those who drag their feet (expect some increasingly painful smacks upside the head if you're a foot-dragger).

TIER 2: The New Opening Business Consultant (NOBC)

Once the pre-opening process is complete, most franchisors will conduct a formal hand-off from the POBC to another consultant who specializes in assisting franchisees during their first year or two in business. As steep as the learning curve is in the pre-opening process, it's even steeper once the business is actually open. This requires a special breed of support person—enter the New Opening Business Consultant, or NOBC. As mentioned earlier, most new franchisees are generally clueless when it comes to running a small business, and many first-year franchisees often have a permanent deer-in-the-headlights look about them. Even if the pre-opening training support was stellar and the POBC did a fabulous job of baby-sitting the franchisee through the process, nothing can truly prepare someone for the first few weeks and/or months in business. It's truly a gut-check experience and a time when many new franchisees will look in the mirror and ask themselves, "What the h-e-double-toothpicks was I thinking?!" Fear not, o frightened reader—the NOBC is here to save the day!

An NOBC's background is often quite varied in that he or she typically is either:

1) A former franchisee/masochist (yuck, yuck)

2) An existing franchisee who is moonlighting and has "volunteered" to help new franchisees get off to a good start (usually in exchange for some form of compensation or concession from the franchisor)

3) An experienced franchise business consultant (FBC) who has held many a hand and wiped many a butt… er…tear while working with brand-new franchisees.

As was the case with the POBC, an NOBC must be able to withstand a tremendous amount of whining and complaining, and in general must possess the hide of a rhinoceros. There's an old saying in the franchising world that goes, "Any success a franchisee achieves is a result of his or her own hard work; any failure is the franchisor's fault." This is what Greg Nathan is referring to in his "Six Stages of the Franchise E-Factor" detailed later in this chapter—specifically, the "fee, me, and free" stages. Trust me—this will all make sense in a few pages.

As you can imagine, the NOBC has to put up with a significant amount of B.S. from new franchisees who are often quick to blame the franchisor for all of their ills. Like a new baby clinging to his or her mother's brea...er...neck, the new franchisee is almost entirely dependent on the franchisor's assistance, which makes for a very interesting dynamic. As the first few weeks and months can quite literally make or break a new franchisee, it is absolutely critical that he or she get off to a strong start. Expect a roller coaster ride during this period and keep a barf bag handy—it *will* get bumpy.

A WARNING

Any franchisor who is more focused on selling new stores than in helping new franchisees to succeed is a franchisor who has his or her priorities seriously screwed up. Although selling new franchises is certainly important, supporting existing (and especially new) franchisees is equally as important, if not more so. Without successful franchisees the entire venture will crumble, which is a mistake made by far too many greedy franchisors who are only interested in their own short-term gain. If you're a new franchisee and you're feeling abandoned and lost, it is *your* responsibility to scream as loudly as necessary to get the attention you deserve. This is one of those times that the squeaky wheel really does get the grease, so go ahead, be a pain the a**—you've paid for that right!

A good NOBC will be in constant communication during the first few weeks after opening, and should generally check in with the new franchisee every other day, or even every day, to make sure things are going smoothly and to answer any questions. During the first few weeks on the job a new franchisee will "touch" every element of the business, and even if the pre-opening training was fantastic, nothing can compare to operating a live business for the first time in the real world. The NOBC needs to be *very* good at addressing high-priority, high-stress situations, and must generally be available virtually 24/7 for the first few weeks/months that a new franchise is open. During the first few weeks/months the learning curve is steepest and this is where a franchisee learns the most. This is also the time when good habits must be formed! Although this may appear to be a relatively minor detail, establishing good habits is arguably one of the most important elements that a franchisee will learn, and is frequently *the* most important contributing factor separating the top franchisees from the rest of the pack. We've all read horror stories about infants who have been abandoned and left in orphanages with no human contact, and the immense physiological and psychological damage that is inflicted. Perhaps my favorite examination of this topic comes from one of my colleagues, Joe Mathews, founding partner of the Franchise Performance Group and a fellow "franchising junkie." In his Developing Peak-Performing Franchisees program, Joe details "The Anatomy of Peak Performance" as follows:

Peak performance happens when franchisees master the K.A.S.H. formula. This formula depends on the application of Knowledge, Attitude, Skills, and Habits to business challenges. Following is how Joe defines each K.A.S.H. element:

Knowledge: Knowledgeable franchisees have high levels of product, service, and operational mastery. They know the business formula inside and out and execute it consistently well over time. Plus, they know how to manage their leverage points, meaning the key activities that produce the greatest results.

Attitude: Franchisees with appropriate attitudes have a realistic and healthy view of their business. Their results may not always be great, but they know why and are working to improve. It is often said that attitude (or thinking), drives all action. Given the same external event (such as political conflict), some attitudes, such as "problem-solving," generate greater results than others, such as "fighting." No one will develop winning habits without first developing winning thoughts. Sound attitude and mental management is key to achieving peak performance.

Skills: Skillful franchisees exhibit polished and effective behaviors on the job. They know how to accomplish their jobs and manage their customers and employees with great effectiveness.

Habits: Franchisees with strong habits produce results easily and naturally. They are almost "unconsciously competent." And they tend to produce more results than do other franchisees with the same time, money, and energy.[7]

Depending on the complexity of the franchise, an NOBC will generally work with a new franchisee from one to two years, and even up to three years in select instances.

TIER 3: The Mature-Owner Business Consultant (MOBC)

Once most franchisees have been in business for a year or two, they've generally figured out the basics of their business and therefore no longer require the level of hand-holding and rudimentary business advice that the NOBC provides. Enter the Mature-Owner Business Consultant, or MOBC. More seasoned franchisees are not necessarily easier franchisees to manage—they just know (or worse, *think* they know), a bit more about what the heck they're doing. Truthfully, this can actually make the MOBC's job even more difficult, because these franchisees frequently believe they know it *all*. Think of this period as the "teen years" in a franchisee's development cycle. These franchisees typically have lots of energy and desire, but they're often headstrong and willful, and will frequently want to "color outside the lines" and be free to do their own thing.

The best explanation I've ever read regarding the lifecycle of the franchisee was created by a guy named Greg Nathan, who wrote the books *The Franchise E-Factor* and *Profitable Partnerships*. I've always been a big fan of Mr. Nathan's work, and in my opinion he is one of the most insightful franchise consultants in the industry (even if he is based "down unda"). The following excerpt from *The Franchise E-Factor*[8] details the classic stages that franchisees in any concept will typically experience to one degree or another. As a former franchisee myself and a guy who's worked with hundreds of franchisees over the years, I can tell you that these developmental stages are remarkably accurate and apply across the board to all franchise concepts.

The six stages of the Franchise E-Factor

GLEE	The franchisee is somewhat nervous about their new venture but is also excited and optimistic about the future.
FEE	The franchisee starts to become sensitive and concerned about the value of the fees being paid to their franchisor or the costs of services or products received.
ME	The franchisee concludes that their success is due mainly to their own effort and plays down the contribution of the franchise system. Or if they are struggling they play down their own deficiencies.
FREE	This stage is characterised by the franchisee's need to demonstrate his or her competence and assert their independence, thus testing the franchise system's boundaries.
SEE	Through frank and open discussions the franchisee and franchisor better understand and respect each other's points of view.
WE	The franchisee recognises that success and satisfaction come more easily from working with, rather than against, their franchisor.

The Six Stages of the Franchise E-Factor

The following graph presents a visual representation of the "Six Stages of the Franchise E-Factor," and clearly demonstrates how franchisee satisfaction declines with time as the franchisee moves from a "dependent" to an "independent" state. It is not until the franchisee transitions to an "interdependent" state (where the franchisee and franchisor are dependent upon one another), that we see satisfaction begin to improve.

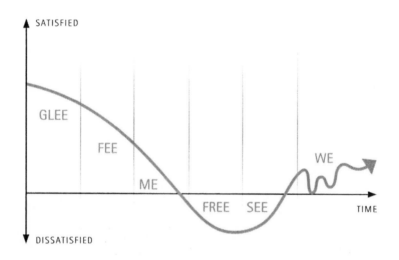

The Six Stages of the Franchise E-Factor Graph
© Copyright Greg Nathan Pty Ltd 2012

Likewise, Joe Mathews in his terrific Developing Peak-Performing Franchisees—Street Smart Training and Support program (as discussed earlier), details a related process Joe refers to as "The Five Phases of the Franchisee Lifecycle." In this graph, Joe describes the five phases as follows:

1) **The Launch:** When a franchisee first signs their franchise agreement, they are filled with mixed emotions. While

there is some fear of the unknown, for the most part they are filled with a sense of joy and empowerment. This is similar to the "Glee" phase described by Greg Nathan.

2) **The Grind:** As franchisees move through what is typically a very steep learning curve, their relationship with their business changes. They begin to come to the realization that owning a franchise is hard work, and their fear of The Launch gives way to the reality of being a small business owner.

3) **Winning:** As franchisees acquire the necessary K.A.S.H. to succeed, they begin to understand that they really can make their business work and they begin to feel a sense of confidence and empowerment.

4) **The Zone:** When franchisees enter The Zone, winning becomes as natural as breathing, and they produce outstanding results as if they were on auto-pilot. The K.A.S.H. success formula has not only been fully internalized and ingrained, it has been systematized and fully realized as a fabric of the culture of the business. Unconscious competence has become habit.

5) **The Goodbye:** In every business lifecycle there will come a time when the owner [franchisee] will conclude that it's time to move on. Typically the franchisee will come to one of two conclusions:

   1. They have accomplished what they originally set out to accomplish and they don't feel that there is anything more to be gained

   2. They *know* they will accomplish everything they set out to accomplish, and although they have not done so yet, they can see the light at the end of the tunnel and it's very bright.[9]

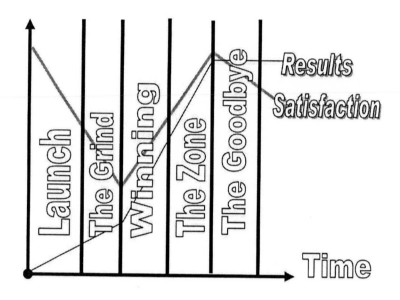

The Five Phases of the Franchisee Lifecycle

Once again, we see that franchisee satisfaction is extremely positive just prior to the launch of the business, then declines precipitously as the franchisee comes to terms with the reality of the daily grind and the massive learning curve he or she is facing. In Joe's graph it's clear that as results improve, the franchisee sees a corresponding improvement in satisfaction. What's unique about Joe's concept is that he actually acknowledges a "goodbye" phase, whereby the franchisee looks to exit the system. Many franchisors are loath to acknowledge that franchisees can, and frequently do, exit franchise systems for myriad reasons. Personally, I believe it's best to acknowledge this fact and to plan for this inevitable transitional period. Franchisors who bury their heads in the sand and ignore the reality that even the best franchisees will eventually move on are simply kidding themselves.

A WARNING FOR FRANCHISEES

A franchisor who does not have a robust and thoroughly vetted resale program is a franchisor who will eventually crash and burn. In my experience, it's not unusual to see up to 15% of the total number of franchise locations up for sale at any one time, so unless the concept you're considering is brand-spanking new, ask about the franchisor's resale program. On the flip side, a franchisor with an unusually high percentage of franchises for sale (20% plus) may be experiencing internal strife, or worse, be more interested in "flipping" franchises than investing in their franchisees' success. Either way, a franchisor's resale program is a good indicator of the overall health and maturity of the operation, so don't overlook this important factor.

The majority of franchisees an MOBC will encounter are probably beginning to experience some level of success, and they tend to be very focused on increasing revenue and decreasing expenses—aka profit! This is a good thing in the franchising world (and in any world for that matter), and many of the best and most innovative ideas will originate from this group. Did you know that the concept of the Big Mac came from a franchisee? How about the Subway® Five-Dollar Foot-Long? Yup, another franchisee-generated idea.

AN IMPORTANT NOTE

The best franchisors *always* take the time listen to their franchisees, because they realize that the vast majority of great ideas will come from those who are out fighting the battle on the front lines.

A WARNING FOR FRANCHISEES

Those franchisors who believe they know it all, or are simply too busy or full of themselves to listen to their franchisees, are almost always a bunch of self-absorbed individuals whose idea of a successful franchise is "Do it my way or hit the highway." This is a major red flag, as any franchisor who is unwilling to listen to a franchisee, is a franchisor who'll also be quick to break out the franchise agreement every time a franchisee steps out of line. This is also known as the "dictatorial" form of franchising and it's *not* a good way to go. Take a good look at Item 3, the litigation section of the FDD, if you ever encounter this type of franchisor. I'd be willing to bet that you'll find a higher than average litigation rate.

Make no mistake, in the world of franchising the golden rule definitely applies: "He who has the gold makes the rules." Just pick up any FDD and you'll quickly determine that the vast majority of these documents are extremely biased in favor of the franchisor. While this is certainly not unusual, it's *how* the FDD is referenced that really matters. As mentioned earlier, those franchisors who feel the need to constantly refer to the FDD and hold it above their franchisees' heads every time they step out of line almost always have a tough time building relationships with their franchisees. If you find that a particular franchise is operated based on a "cult of personality" (which is typically the founder) and the founder is an egomaniac, watch out!

TIER 4: The Very-Mature-Owner Business Consultant (VMOBC)

Typically, only larger franchisors (300-plus units) will have Very-Mature-Owner Business Consultants (VMOBC's), because VMOBC's typically work solely with franchisees who have been in business for a minimum of four to five years. A very mature franchisee is frequently extremely comfortable with his or her chosen business, and generally operates at an entirely different level than the "average" franchisee. Very mature franchisees are often either multi-unit owners or are seeking to become multi-unit owners, and their challenges frequently involve more complex strategic and logistical issues. The VMOBC's often were (or in some cases still are) multi-unit franchisees themselves, and they typically have direct, hands-on experience in dealing with more sophisticated and complex issues. In more mature franchising organizations, it's not unusual to have a small number of multi-unit franchisees who control a large number of units, which can be both a blessing and a curse.

A WARNING FOR FRANCHISORS

Very mature multi-unit franchisees can, and often do, amass a tremendous amount of power and wealth. It's not unusual in these situations for a mature franchisee to begin thinking that he or she is "above the law" when it comes to the franchise agreement and the goals of the franchisor, which can be extremely damaging to the franchise system as a whole. It can be very difficult to rein in these types of franchisees once they begin to flex their muscles, so often the best solution is to listen to them and *keep them engaged.*

Perhaps the best way to ensure that all parties are on the same page with regard to the direction of the franchise concept and any key initiatives is to create a franchise advisory council, or FAC. The FAC is formed by the franchisor, and will typically include a formal charter as well as an approved set of bylaws. The FAC is generally operated and moderated by the franchisor's president and/or vice president of operations, along with a number of appointed or elected delegates from the franchise community.

When an FAC is first formed, the first group of franchisee delegates is often hand-picked by the franchisor, and will serve as the "founding member group." In more mature FAC's, these members (or delegates) are often voted onto the FAC by their peers (the franchisees themselves), in an effort to ensure a fair and unbiased representation of the franchise system. Typically, the number of FAC franchisees selected will range from five to as many as eight, and will represent a broad cross-section of the franchise community, including "New Opening" franchisees (less than one year of experience), "Mature" franchisees (one year to three years of experience), and "Very Mature" franchisees (four-plus years of experience). If possible, the franchise representatives should also represent different geographic areas of the country (or the world for international franchisors), as well as different socioeconomic levels (blue-collar, white-collar, etc.).

FAC's often meet in person on a quarterly basis for at least one or two days, and each meeting is based on a formal agenda of topics ranging from operations to franchise development to marketing. (In my opinion, the best FAC's are operated based on the parliamentary procedure detailed in the "gold standard" of meeting procedure books, *Robert's Rules of Order*. (Originally published as a slim document in 1896, General Henry M. Robert's guide to smooth, orderly, and fairly conducted meetings has sold close to five million copies in nine editions.) These FAC meetings are frequently supplemented in the interim months with phone calls and/or webinars. The agenda may also include any of the other Ten Key Elements of Franchising (see Chapter 1), along with a host of other topics. The FAC provides both the franchisees and the franchisor the opportunity to share their thoughts, opinions, and ideas in an open and collaborative format, and can play a critical role in the success of any franchising organization.

AN IMPORTANT NOTE

The FAC is NOT typically a governing body, but rather an advisory group. Although a good franchisor will encourage healthy dialogue and an environment where ideas are shared freely, any and all decisions that the FAC makes are subject to the final approval of the franchisor and are not binding on

> the franchisor. In other words, the franchisor retains the right to make any and all decisions regarding the direction of the franchise. There's a reason it's called a franchise *advisory* council. Make no mistake, franchisors want to maintain absolute control of their brand and systems, and although good franchisors really do care about their franchisees' opinions and interests, unfortunately, I have heard many a franchisee utter something along the lines of, "It's a franchisor's world and we're just livin' in it."

Along these lines, although it's a fact that the balance of power in the franchising world has traditionally been heavily skewed in favor of the franchisor, many franchisees have begun to wake up to the fact that they too should have rights, and one organization in particular, the American Association of Franchisees and Dealers (AAFD), has become quite vocal in this arena.

THE AAFD

So what the heck is the AAFD and why are they so hell-bent on promoting the rights of franchisees? Well, to put it simply, the AAFD, headed by Robert L. Purvin, Chairman and CEO, believes that franchisees have gotten a raw deal for a very long time, and as longtime news anchor Howard Beale declared in Sydney Lumet's masterpiece of cinematic satire *Network* (1976), "I'm as mad as hell, and I'm not going to take this anymore!"

THE BACKGROUND

Over the past 50 years the concept of franchising has grown to become of the most powerful methods ever conceived for the distribution of products and services. Tens of thousands of companies around the globe have adopted the franchising business model, and correspondingly, millions of individuals have made the decision to operate franchise businesses encompassing virtually every conceivable concept—from fast food to dog poop removal (I kid you not).

As the idea of franchising exploded, so did the wealth associated with it, and in the U.S. franchising has evolved into an 800-billion-dollar-a-year money-making juggernaut. Naturally, as franchising took off and became mainstream, it began to attract a tremendous amount of attention—some of it good, and some of it not so good. As with any capitalist venture, there are those who believe in the "everyone should win philosophy," and those who believe that they themselves must win at any cost and to the detriment of others. It's the latter that the AAFD is fighting against—and in my personal opinion, with good cause. I began this book by stating that I firmly believe franchising must be a win-win for both parties, and I will end this book with the same statement. The AAFD believes, as stated in their website, that "…as the franchising community has experienced explosive growth, franchisors have learned they need promise very little in order to attract buyers." In addition, they believe that "a 'seller's market' in franchising has led to a serious decline in the quality of franchise opportunities" and that "the problems in franchising are all directly related to the inability of the marketplace to recognize unfair franchising practices, and to demand better product from franchisors."[10]

So what do the members of the AAFD believe is the answer to fixing what they clearly perceive as a broken system? The answer can be summed up in two programs: 1) Total Quality Franchising; and 2) the AAFD Franchisee Bill of Rights. I believe it's worthwhile to briefly examine these two concepts, as I feel very strongly that the hue and cry regarding the concept of franchisee rights will only increase over the next few years.

TOTAL QUALITY FRANCHISING

Total Quality Franchising, or "TQF," is rooted in the core belief that individually franchisees are weak, but together they can be incredibly strong. As such, the AAFD firmly believes franchisors must recognize that franchisees have the right to form an independent association, and that franchisors must understand that "the best franchise systems are built through the collaborative and negotiated efforts of franchise systems in which franchisors and franchisees have formed strong bonds of respect and mutual support for the overall success of the network and business of the system."[11] In other words, although the AAFD is certainly not positioning themselves as "anti-franchisor," they believe that the best way to ensure that the needs and wants of franchisees are acknowledged, is to form an independent association, which, by the way, is a service they will gladly provide for a fee.

What's interesting about the AAFD and similar organizations is that while the concept of collective bargaining has been around for hundreds of years, it really hasn't gained a foothold in the world of franchising until relatively recently. As the economy continues to limp along and small-business owners are increasingly feeling the pinch, I have absolutely no doubt that more and more franchisees will seek safety in numbers.

THE AAFD FRANCHISEE BILL OF RIGHTS

For many franchisors (or future franchisors) who are under the impression that franchising is a quick and easy road to riches where the franchisor calls all the shots and the franchisees follow along like good little soldiers, the AAFD's message is absolutely terrifying. The very thought of franchisees banding together in organized groups to fight for what they believe in is, for most franchisors, tantamount to mutiny or treason, and many would do just about anything in their power to quickly quell any such uprising. That being said, those franchisors who understand that "all boats rise together" will, on the whole, not fear an independent franchisee organization, and the most enlightened may actually come to welcome the input and unique perspective of an independent association.

Perhaps one of the best illustrations of the AAFD's perspective is the Franchisee Bill of Rights, which is one of the foundational tenets of the AAFD's TQF program, and represents, in the AAFD's opinion, the minimum requirements of a fair and equitable franchise system.

- *The right to an equity in the franchised business, including the right to meaningful market protection.*

- *The right to engage in a trade or business, including a post-termination right to compete.*

- *The right to the franchisors loyalty, good faith and fair dealing, and due care in the performance of the franchisors duties, and a fiduciary relationship where one has been promised or created by conduct.*

- *The right to trademark protection.*

- *The right to full disclosure from the franchisor, including the right to earnings data available to the franchisor which is relevant to the franchisees decision to enter or remain in the franchise relationship.*

- *The right to initial and ongoing training and support.*

- *The right to competitive sourcing of inventory, product, service and supplies.*

- *The right to reasonable restraints upon the franchisors ability to require changes within the franchise system.*

- *The right to marketing assistance.*

- *The right to associate with other franchisees.*

- *The right to representation and access to the franchisor.*

- *The right to local dispute resolution and protection under the laws and the courts of the franchisee's jurisdiction.*

- *A reasonable right to review the franchise.*

- *The reciprocal right to terminate the franchise agreement for reasonable and just cause, and the right not to face termination, unless for cause.*

The AAFD Franchisee Bill of Rights

Every time I read the Franchisee Bill of Rights, all I can say to myself is, "Wow." For those of you who have never been a franchisor or worked for one, let me just say that in my humble opinion this is quite possibly one of the most controversial documents I have ever come across. Please don't misunderstand me—it is not my intention to disparage this document in any way, and I am not an AAFD detractor by any means. It's just that knowing how most franchisors think and behave (as I do), if a group franchisees who recently banded together to form an independent franchisee association marched into their franchisor's headquarters, presented this document to the president and said, "This is what we want," the %$@# storm this would likely cause would be...well...let's just say on a scale of one to 10, it would be a 12. I think the franchisor's president would jump out of his or her chair so quickly that a new land speed record would be set.

While I believe that several of the items in the Franchisee Bill of Rights would be considered quite controversial from a franchisor perspective, I would *strongly* recommend that all franchisors (or perspective franchisors) spend some time browsing the AAFD's website. You may not necessarily like what you see, but burying your head in the sand or wishing that it would just go away is not a strategy that I would recommend.

CHAPTER NOTES

CHAPTER 3: ELEMENT II

7, 9) Developing Peak-Performing Franchisees, Street Smart Franchising for Franchisees, by Joe Mathews, Franchise Performance Group, © 2006 Joe Mathews and The Franchise Performance Group

8) *The Franchise E-Factor*, copyright 2004 Greg Nathan Pty Ltd, Franchise Relationships Institute, PO Box 233, Toowong Queensland, Australia 4066, www.franchiserelationships.com

10, 11) © 1996-2011 American Association of Franchisees & Dealers, All Rights Reserved www.aafd.org/the-aafd-story/

Chapter 4
Element III: Training

So how does a franchisor go about transforming an eager new franchisee into a sophisticated, successful business owner? Why, training, of course! As mentioned previously, the learning curve for new franchisees is very steep, and most franchisees feel like they're drinking from a fire hose. It's important to keep in mind that the franchisor has a tremendous amount of information to cram into a franchisee's brain in a relatively short period of time, so the vast majority of (good) franchisors will integrate the training schedule into the pre-opening timeline to ensure that the correct information is presented at the optimal time. This is not necessarily an easy thing to do. If the training occurs too early, the data will probably be forgotten. If the training occurs too late, the franchisee may not have enough time to properly absorb and process the information, which usually leads to execution-related challenges. Most franchisors will utilize some combination of in-house training (corporate headquarters) and field training (on-site at a company-owned or franchisee-owned location). This is frequently supplemented with web (e-learning), phone, and/or webinar-based training.

FRANCHISE TRAINING – CONTENT

From a content perspective, a robust franchise training program should always include everything a franchisee needs to know about the specific product and/or service being provided. Truthfully, a good training program should include *all* of the Ten Key Elements of Franchising, as franchisees will need to be competent in all of these areas if they're going to succeed. Although much of the information that would be included in a good training program is addressed in the various chapters of this book, let's take a closer look at two of the ten key elements of franchising as they apply to franchisee training—franchise sales and operations.

FRANCHISE SALES

Knowing how to sell your product or service is one of the most basic elements of success for any franchisee. Far too many franchisees fail because they just don't understand the fundamental difference between taking an order and selling. In basic terms, *selling* is what a franchisee must do to motivate a customer to purchase a good or a service that the customer did not proactively request. *Order taking* is simply satisfying a request for a particular good or service. Here's a real-world example from my time spent in the world of automotive service and repair.

Order Taking:

> Customer: "Hello, Mr. Serviceman. I've been driving around on bald tires for a couple of months now and I've decided that I need four new tires. I've done a lot of research and I want the Good Brand tires. Can you have my car ready by three p.m.?"

Mr. Serviceman: "Yes."

Customer: "Great, here are my keys—see you at three."

Selling:

Customer: "Hello, Mr. Serviceman. I've been driving around on bald tires for a couple of months now and I've decided that I need four new tires. I've done a lot of research and I want the Good Brand tires. Can you have my car ready by three p.m.?"

Mr. Serviceman: "Sure, I have the Good Brand tires in stock; however, I'd strongly recommend that we also take care of the balancing, alignment, and road hazard for you. This will not only prolong the life of your tires, but you'll get better gas mileage as well, and who doesn't want that?"

Customer: "Sounds good. Why don't you take care of that for me as well. See you at three."

Mr. Serviceman: "See you then!" (And to himself, *Cha-ching!*)

If a franchisee does not come out of training knowing how to *sell* the product or service being offered, then the franchising system is fundamentally flawed. A good training program should include role-playing, script memorization, and anything else that will aid in the selling process.

OPERATIONS

The key to a successful training program is a robust and well-crafted operations manual. A good operations manual should be written from the perspective of a franchisee who has absolutely no experience in the business he or she has purchased. Every single step in the development of a new business should be documented, beginning with the most basic such as finding a site, opening a bank account, obtaining a federal tax identification number, and even implementing general good business practices. The operations manual should also include legal elements such as labor and wage laws, EEOC, sexual harassment, the Americans with Disabilities Act, and a variety of other laws that are relevant to small businesses. And, of course, the operations manual must include very specific instructions regarding the operations of the business, reporting requirements, and expected standards of performance.

The balance of the Ten Key Elements of Franchising—real estate, equipment/merchandise, finance/accounting, marketing, human resources, information technology, and legal—should all be addressed in the training process as well. The material to be covered from a content standpoint in any training program is addressed in later chapters of this book.

FRANCHISE TRAINING – FORMAT

From a format perspective, a strong franchise training program should always include the following:

- franchise support center (headquarters) training

- internship/mentor program

- on-site training

- ongoing training

Franchise Support Center (Headquarters) Training

One key element of almost all franchise training programs involves training at the franchisor's headquarters. A good franchisor must first develop a formal training agenda for the franchise's pre-opening training course at headquarters. While the operations manual should serve as the primary "textbook" throughout the training program, the agenda should contain the broad list of topics that extend beyond the scope of the manual itself.

Internship/Mentor Program

So how do doctors learn how to work with patients and hospital staff in a real-world setting before they're allowed to practice on their own? Why, in an internship, of course! Doctors learn by observing and doing and getting their hands dirty, and by teaching others what they've learned. So what's the best way to ensure that a new franchisee truly understands his or her business *before* picking up a bunch of bad habits or making a number of costly mistakes? You guessed it—an internship. Many of the best franchisors now require their franchisees to spend time (often one or two weeks) working as an "employee" at one of their top franchise locations, so they can really understand how the business works from the inside out. This practice has multiple benefits:

1) It ensures that the franchisee has the opportunity to understand the business in a real-world scenario (which is invaluable), because no amount of role-play can ever duplicate a live business setting.

2) It helps the franchisee establish a relationship with a mentor-franchisee, and sets the groundwork for a long and healthy franchisee partnership.

3) It allows the mentor-franchisee to observe the pre-opening franchisee in action, and to provide feedback to the franchisor regarding any necessary course corrections.

4) By closely observing the mentor-franchisee in action (who, by the way, is always a top-ranked franchisee), the pre-opening franchisee learns good habits early, which is the "H" component of the K.A.S.H. model as discussed in Element II: Operations.

On-site Training

On-site training is an extremely important element of the training process as well, as this is typically the first time a new franchisee has the opportunity to actually work in his or her own business. It also happens to be one of the most exciting times in a franchisee's career, and contributes significantly to the "glee" phase of a franchisee's lifecycle (see Element II: Operations).

As with the franchise support center training, a franchisor should develop a detailed training agenda for the on-site training program. Given the fact that the training will take place on-site at the franchisee's location, the training should focus on topics that assist the franchisee in becoming more familiar and comfortable with the day-to-day operation of the business.

Ongoing Training

While the majority of franchisors provide extensive training to new franchisees, many do a poor job when it comes to ensuring that existing franchisees receive ongoing and refresher training. To ensure that system standards are maintained and that all franchisees are exposed to the latest and greatest in franchise products and services, franchisors should develop ongoing certification programs that incorporate a testing-for-competence component. By testing franchisees (and managers) on a regular basis, a franchisor will be in a much better position to assess the overall health of his or her system, and correspondingly, will be able to develop new training materials to address any deficiencies.

AN IMPORTANT NOTE FOR FRANCHISEES

Training is not something that a franchisee must "survive"—nor is it an expensive working vacation. A franchisor's training program can literally make or break a franchisee, so it's *critical* that a franchisee soak in every second of training. Remember, over the course of a typical franchise term a franchisee will pay tens (or even hundreds) of thousands of dollars in royalties to learn how to make the "secret sauce," so squandering this opportunity is just plain dumb.

AN INTERESTING NOTE

An increasing number of franchisors are migrating to web-based (aka e-learning) training platforms to provide on-demand training to their franchisees. Web-based training allows franchisees and employees to access critical information, learn new skills, and refresh existing knowledge in a self-paced, user-friendly format. This can be beneficial to both franchisors and franchisees in that:

1. An educated workforce improves performance and customer satisfaction

2. Professional development can help reduce employee turnover

3. Training costs can be significantly reduced (travel, personnel, etc.)

4. New information can be communicated efficiently and effectively across an entire system instantly

Keep an eye out for franchisors offering these types of tools, as this is generally an indication that the franchisor "gets it" and is willing and able to invest in his or her future and the future of his or her franchisees.

Chapter 5
Element IV: Real Estate

In many franchising organizations, the real estate department plays a key role in helping franchisees with their needs relating to market analysis, site selection, lease negotiation, unit build-out (construction), and market development. Larger, more established franchisors generally have an in-house real estate team, while smaller franchisors may either have one real estate specialist on-site or, in some cases, outsource the entire real estate function to a third party.

The real estate department generally serves three basic purposes:

1) To help identify a suitable physical location (or locations) for each unit and/or to vet an existing location identified by a franchisee.

2) To assist with the build-out phase to ensure the location is built according to an established timeline and to the specifications stipulated by the franchisor.

3) To facilitate (or provide advice and guidance regarding) the lease and/or purchase of the facility to ensure that the tenant (franchisee) remains in compliance with the terms of the lease.

ITEM 1: LOCATION ANALYSIS

Regardless of whether you're planning to lease an existing location or build a new location from the ground up, locating a suitable site at the right price has significant ramifications for both the franchisee and franchisor. For the franchisee, real estate represents one of the most important financial investments the franchisee will make, and can significantly help or hinder a business.

AN IMPORTANT NOTE FOR FRANCHISEES

From an operational perspective, most franchisees do not need to build or lease a "Taj Mahal" location. Many eager new (read: clueless) franchisees are so excited about their shiny new business that they can't wait to show it off to all their friends and family. "Look how cool/smart/rich I am! Doesn't my new [insert name of franchise here] franchise look amazing?" Epilogue: 12 months later they are either out of business or desperately trying to sell at a huge loss. It happens all the time.

Unless your franchisor specifically states that you are required to spend a small fortune on your location, and/or that you must be located in an "A" territory (prime, high-traffic area), you will generally be much better off leasing (or in some cases building) a nice, professional-looking space in a "B" or "C" location. Don't believe me? Just ask your accountant to run a few P&L scenarios based on several high-, medium-, and low-rent factors and you'll quickly see that I speak the truth. Having an enormous monthly rent can be both daunting and depressing, and it can add a tremendous amount of pressure to an already stressful situation (being a new business owner is a scary undertaking, folks).

A WARNING FOR FRANCHISEES

Commercial real estate is not a game, nor is it something to be taken lightly. DO NOT make the mistake of overestimating your brilliance in this area. If you do not have much (or any) experience in this arena—and most people don't—by all means hire a competent professional to negotiate on your behalf! Yes, I know money is tight, but now is not the time to be penny-wise and pound-foolish. Are you really planning to spend thousands of dollars on that beautiful brand-new cherry and marble front desk, but you won't shell out a few bucks on a competent and experienced commercial real estate expert? Not smart...and a classic rookie mistake.

A WORD TO THE WISE

I've personally worked with a number of very competent third-party "hired gun" real estate negotiators, and I've seen them save tens of thousands of dollars in rent concessions and tenant improvements simply by knowing the right questions to ask. And as a rule, the savings gained by using a professional franchise lease negotiator will far exceed the costs, so don't be a cheapskate—make the investment!

ITEM 2: THE BUILD-OUT

One of the keys to operating a successful franchising organization is an unwavering quest for uniformity across the system, which is why many franchisors are such sticklers when it comes to the build-out of each location. In fact, some franchisors are so particular about their facilities that once a suitable site is located, the entire build-out, from soup to nuts, is completed by either an internal construction department or, more frequently, by a contracted third-party construction firm. In the latter scenario, the franchisee simply shows up one day, puts his or her key in the front door, and presto: instant franchise! Just know that while this turnkey process certainly minimizes the risk of non-conformity, it can be quite costly, and guess what? It's not the franchisor who's footing the bill.

For those franchisees who are stuck with the unenviable task of building out their chosen location themselves, a good franchisor will ensure that his or her internal real estate department (or person) is along for the ride every step of the way and available to provide assistance and input as necessary. A good franchisor will also generally require proof that certain key benchmarks have been met, such as the receipt of a certificate of occupancy (aka C of O, or just CO). Most franchisors will also require either photos or video detailing the build-out process, and a final inspection by either a designated real estate employee or a POBC.

Construction

As is the case with real estate, the construction process can be fraught with challenges (and scam artists), so a good franchisor will either have his or her own team of experts on hand, or access to an experienced project manager via a third-party relationship to coordinate all the pieces and keep everyone honest.

A WARNING

If you think you've met some contemptible people in the commercial real estate industry, just wait until you have to deal with some of the general contractors (aka GC's) out there. Though most GC's are reputable and will do a fair and honest job, construction cost overruns can quickly eat into your working capital and drain you of critical resources. A beautiful facility is worthless if you've just blown your entire marketing budget to make it happen, so keep a close eye on your pocketbook and an even closer eye on your contractors!

The Location Lease

In general, only the larger franchisors actually own their real estate or lease specific locations on behalf of their franchisees. For some gigantic franchisors (such as McDonald's), their real estate portfolio can actually be worth more than the entire franchise operation itself; however, these franchisors are in an entirely different league, and their in-house real estate departments are essentially equivalent to the best commercial real estate and construction companies around.

Some franchisors prefer to lease their locations themselves, and in turn sub-lease the locations back to their franchisees. For these franchisors, the attraction is two-fold: 1) the ability to have complete control of the lease terms and transaction, and 2) to be able to retain the site if the franchisee bails out or is terminated. This can be a risky move for franchisors, as they bear all the risk if the franchisee doesn't work out; however, these types of franchisors are generally confident that they will be able to either secure another franchisee quickly or operate the unit as a company-owned store if things go sideways.

Smaller and/or newer franchisors who aren't comfortable signing a lease on behalf of their franchisees often will add an addendum to their franchise agreement stating that in the event of a termination or failure, the franchisor will be granted a specific period of time (such as 30 days) during which he or she has the first right of refusal to accept, reject, or re-negotiate the existing lease. During this time, the landlord is prohibited from leasing the location to another individual or entity, which provides some breathing room for the franchisor to decide how to handle the situation. In other instances, the franchisor may agree to simply step into the franchisee's shoes as the lessee in the event of a default. And finally, some franchisors want nothing to do with a franchisee's lease, which, by the way, was one of the original proclaimed benefits of franchising—that the franchisor did not incur the lease obligations of the individual franchisees.

AN INTERESTING NOTE

The topic of franchisors' involvement in their franchisees' real estate has become somewhat contentious during the past few years, as proponents and opponents on both sides of the fence have voiced their opinions. Franchisors have typically argued that their ability to maintain control of their franchisees' real estate is critical for three primary reasons: 1) They want to be able to enforce non-competition restraints in the event of a default or termination, 2) they want the right to exercise control of a valuable location that has amassed significant goodwill as a result of leveraging the franchisor's trademarks and intellectual property, and 3) in the event of a franchisee lease default, they want to ensure that they receive timely notification from the landlord. On the other side, some pro-franchisee forces have argued that franchisors' desires to control their franchisees' real estate is simply a thinly veiled attempt to further dominate the franchisor/franchisee relationship by effectively tying the real estate to the franchise agreement. Essentially, a violation of the franchise agreement would constitute a violation of the lease, which means bye-bye franchise location, and therefore, so long franchisee livelihood.

The truth of the matter is that *both* the franchisee and the franchisor have valid reasons for wanting to protect their respective interests, and there are advantages and disadvantages in each scenario. What's most important is that in a healthy franchisor/franchisee relationship, all parties must work together to ensure a balanced and equitable solution for the benefit of all.

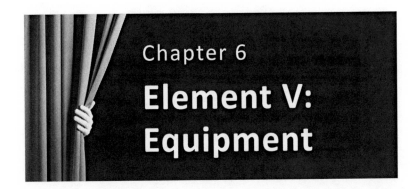

Chapter 6

Element V: Equipment

The equipment package is often included as a component of the construction process, and can either be a major pain or simple and hassle-free. I don't know about you, but personally, I prefer the latter. Most established franchisors have moved to a store-in-a-box model, whereby everything a store needs is prepackaged by the franchisor (or a third party) and delivered to the location in a nice, neat, organized process. This concept is especially well-suited to the franchising environment, based on the strong need for consistency from location to location.

AN IMPORTANT NOTE

Assembling all of the items necessary to implement a store-in-a-box concept is neither easy nor inexpensive, and the franchisor will very likely pass along these costs to the franchisee. As such, the franchisor will typically add a markup to the cost (generally on the order of 10%), as the sale of an equipment package can serve as a nice little profit center for a franchisor. These markups are not necessarily unreasonable or unethical (although organizations such as the AAFD will expect (or demand) full transparency on behalf of the franchisor); however, if you're a franchisee and you're wondering why your franchisor won't allow you to purchase the identical inventory online (for less), this is most likely the primary reason. To be fair, franchisors do have a legitimate need to ensure like kind and quality when it comes to their build-outs, and if asked politely, most franchisors will at least consider an outside purchase, although I wouldn't hold my breath.

Merchandise

Not all franchisors will have a merchandise and inventory department, but those who do must ensure that the merchandise they stock and provide their franchisees is of the highest quality and assorted properly at the store level. One could easily write an entire book about merchandising and the how's and why's of effective wholesale and retail product management, but I am not that guy. Let's just say that for those franchisors who rely on selling products to their franchisees, all supply-chain channels must be efficient and robust, and products must be priced correctly (and fairly) from a wholesale perspective.

> ## ⚠ A WARNING FOR FRANCHISORS
>
> Many greedy franchisors have gotten themselves into hot water by mandating that their franchisees purchase various goods from them based on a ridiculously high markup. While it's perfectly reasonable to build in a profit margin on the sale of goods to franchisees, it's simply unethical to gouge franchisees simply because the FDD stipulates that the franchisee must purchase his or her merchandise and inventory from the franchisor. Remember the American Association of Franchisees and Dealers' Franchisee Bill of Rights from Element II? Well, this is one of those issues that the AAFD is not shy about addressing, so franchisors beware: Exorbitant markups can and most likely will come back to haunt you.

I have personally been involved in a number of situations where franchisees have requested, or more accurately demanded, to know exactly how much their franchisor was marking up their merchandise and equipment. In every instance the franchisor immediately provided this information, which: 1) diffused the situation, and 2) led to some very productive FAC discussions. Following is a great example of this topic:

> Last November, when an Illinois federal court preliminarily approved a $100 million settlement resolving four class action lawsuits filed by certain Quiznos franchisees against the Quiznos organization, the franchisees involved, as well as all existing and potential Quiznos franchisees, reaped the financial benefits of the settlement

and the benefits of an agreement by Quiznos to be more transparent with respect to its supply chain. Specifically, Quiznos agreed to submit to an annual review of its supply and food prices by a third-party auditor and to revise its Franchise Disclosure Document (FDD) to clarify the supply chain disclosure and the involvement of Quiznos-owned entities.

The Quiznos class actions included claims of fraud, antitrust, racketeering and violations of applicable state franchise, business opportunity and consumer protection laws. The plaintiffs alleged that Quiznos required franchisees to purchase food and supplies from Quiznos or its affiliates and then improperly inflated prices on food and supplies to amounts much higher than franchisees would pay comparable suppliers, with Quiznos receiving significant rebates from these affiliates on franchisee food and supply purchases. The plaintiffs also alleged that the rebates and Quiznos' supplier relationships were not properly disclosed in Item 8 of the Quiznos FDD.

Supply chain issues and allegations of inflated food prices by franchisees had plagued Quiznos for years, and such issues are frequently the focus of franchisee ire in other franchise systems, particularly in the restaurant industry. With the Quiznos settlement, however, the franchisees finally saw results, which likely will prompt and, in at least one case, already has prompted franchisees in other systems to bring similar claims against their franchisors.[12]

As discussed in Element II: Operations, organizations such as the AAFD are rapidly increasing in both strength and numbers. Franchisors would be well advised to ensure a greater degree of transparency when it comes to issues such as supply chain and supply sourcing. After all, the seventh bullet point in the AAFD's Franchisee Bill of Rights reads, "The right to competitive sourcing of inventory, product, service and supplies." Greedy franchisors—you've been warned.

CHAPTER NOTES
CHAPTER 6: ELEMENT V

12) Newsletter—"Hospitalitas" 2010 Issue 2, Jillian M. Suwanski, April 14, 2010, http://www.bakerdonelson. com/quiznos-settlement-quiznos-settlement-on-supply-chain-issues-04-14-2010/

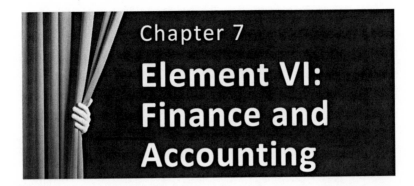

Chapter 7

Element VI: Finance and Accounting

A h, the joys of the finance and accounting department. Those happy-go-lucky bean counters. (Sorry, CFO's/ accountants out there—I'm just joshing.) Truthfully, I have been fortunate in my career in that the vast majority of financial professionals I've worked with have been extremely capable, competent, and well-educated.

In most franchising organizations, the finance and accounting department serves four basic functions:

BASIC FUNCTION ONE: COLLECTIONS

To collect and account for ALL monies owed by the franchisees for everything, from the initial franchise fee to the monthly royalties to the marketing fund payments to the annual convention attendance fee. You get the idea. While the collection of various franchise fees may at first blush appear to be a no-brainer, don't be fooled—this is not always the case.

Many people believe that the initial franchise fee a franchisor collects goes straight to the franchisor's bottom line; however, this is actually far from the truth. For most franchisors, the franchise fee is almost entirely allocated to the acquisition of new franchisees. Between the commissions paid to the franchise development department and the marketing costs associated with acquiring new franchisees, there is often nothing left over for the franchisor once these are paid. The *real* money in franchising comes from the royalty fees generated by the operating franchisees, so as you can imagine, the collection of these fees is a *very* high priority for franchisors.

Although many franchisors do a reasonably solid job of enforcing royalty collections, there are certainly plenty who don't, and these franchisors can get into some deep sh…uh, doo-doo very quickly. In a well-run franchise, royalty payments are considered sacrosanct and not to be messed with. If a franchisee misses a payment, the franchisor will typically immediately send out a notice informing the franchisee that he or she is in default of the franchise agreement (this is also known as a notice of default). This notice includes a specific time period in which to cure the default. If this sounds like legal jargon, you're right—it is.

When a franchisor sends out a communication to a franchisee that includes legalese, this is rarely, if ever, a good thing, and a franchisee had better sit up and pay attention. While some franchisors may offer a grace period during which the franchisee may cure the default, others may take a much harder line and may even move to terminate the franchise agreement if they're motivated to do so. Good franchisors know that if they become lax in their royalty collection efforts things can go south very quickly, and many a franchisor has wound up with massive collection issues as a result of being too lenient in royalty collections. Royalties are not a joke, so if you're a franchisee, pay them promptly. If you are unable to make a payment, it's always best to take a proactive approach in contacting the franchisor, as this will demonstrate a commitment to the process and a level of professionalism that the franchisor will most likely respect and appreciate.

A WARNING

I've worked with franchisors who have entire departments devoted solely to collecting delinquent royalties. These royalty collectors, aka accounts receivable or A/R collectors, are essentially debt collectors/repo men, and they will frequently engage in cat-and-mouse games with franchisees in an effort to collect past-due franchise fees and related debts. I've personally witnessed many of these collection shenanigans, and let me tell you, it's not pretty. If a franchisor gets to the point where this process becomes a standard operating procedure, watch out—this is a huge red flag for both the franchisor and franchisee.

BASIC FUNCTION TWO: ACCOUNTING

The accounting function exists to ensure that the books are balanced, taxes are paid, etc. Like any business, a franchisor exists to make money, and as such, revenue must be tracked, expenses managed, and profits maximized. A franchisor with a weak accounting department is asking for trouble, so maybe there's a reason why so many CFO's have such a low tolerance for BS.

In addition, the finance and accounting department provides support with equipment invoicing, accounts receivable (A/R), accounts payable (A/P), collections, and the collection and allocation of the marketing fund.

BASIC FUNCTION THREE: FINANCING

The financing function supports franchisee financing as it relates to the purchase of the franchise itself, equipment purchases, etc. During the last few years, franchise financing has played an increasingly important role for many franchisors, and there's a saying in franchising that says, "So goes financing, so goes franchise sales." For many franchisees the ability to obtain financing can mean the difference between actually becoming a franchisee and sitting at home dreaming about becoming a franchisee. The franchise financing field has exploded in recent years. As the financial markets around the world continue to struggle and the U.S. credit markets have largely dried up (as of this printing), many financing organizations have been looking to alternative financing methods such as 401(k)'s and "angel" financing, as well as the Small Business Administration (SBA), which has played an active role in franchise lending.

Although some of the larger franchisors have made the decision to offer internal (self) financing programs to their franchisees, most franchisors simply do not have the resources to self-fund, so most rely on relationships with a number of institutions and business partners. Following is a summary of a few of the most common financing relationships:

FUNDING SOURCES

Self-Funding

If you have the cash or if you can beg, borrow, or steal from your family and friends, this can sometimes be a viable option.

Home Equity

If you happen to be one of the fortunate few who still has any home equity, this is still a viable option for funding a franchise.

Just keep in mind that home-equity lending programs can vary greatly, so always read the fine print.

Retirement Funds

If you're really brave and are willing to risk your future (literally), you can consider tapping into your 401(k) or other retirement sources. Many financing companies have become very creative in this space, so you may want to surf on over to the International Franchise Association's website at www.franchise.org, and check out their list of "suppliers" under their "resources" tab.

Conventional Lenders

While it will most likely be very challenging to secure funding through a "traditional" large lender, such as Bank of America or Wells Fargo, these days, you may have some luck approaching credit unions and various local and regional banks.

The Small Business Administration (SBA)

Although the SBA is not a lender, it does guarantee a large percentage of a business loan, which generally makes banks feel more comfortable about lending. To learn more about the SBA packages you can visit www.sba.gov.

The Franchise Registry

I have personal experience with the Franchise Registry, which can streamline the SBA lending process for a franchisee and serve as a nice little value-added service for a franchisor. It can also increase the credibility of the franchisor in the eyes of many banks. Loan applications for franchisors listed on the SBA's Franchise Registry can be processed more quickly by the

SBA and its lenders (banks), because the SBA has pre-approved the franchisor's franchise agreement.

A NOTE FOR FRANCHISORS

If you're a franchisor, it will likely take any-where from 14 to 16 weeks to become an approved franchise registry entity, so be prepared for a long haul. Visit www.franchiseregistry.com to learn more.

Business Partner or Investor

Although your initial vision may have been to "go it alone" in your new franchise venture, sometimes spreading the risk around with a little diversification goes a long way. If you can find someone who wants to become a partner (either active or silent), or perhaps someone who's just looking to invest a few bucks, bringing on another person can sometimes lighten the load significantly. Just be very careful about partnering with friends and family. Many relationships have been destroyed as a direct result of a failed business venture, so choose your partners wisely.

Franchisors

Given the distress in the lending markets, many of the larger franchisors have begun self-funding programs for their franchisees. Just as it sounds, these franchisors are essentially acting as lenders, and financing their franchisees' purchases. These types of arrangements are usually found in franchises that require a substantial investment ($300,000 and more), and are most often found in the restaurant or hospitality industries.[13]

A Really Interesting New Product – Personal Guarantee Insurance™

One of the biggest fears for any franchisee (or any business owner for that matter), is signing a personal guarantee for a commercial loan. A personal guarantee is just what it sounds like: a guarantee from the person soliciting a loan, credit, or contract on behalf of his or her business entity (LLC, S-corp, etc.) to repay the loan. The person making the personal guarantee (the guarantor) is essentially pledging all of his or her personal assets (home, cars, bank accounts, etc.) as collateral against the loan. It's essentially the equivalent of signing a blank check without a date, and it can be terrifying for any franchisee. In an effort to mitigate some of this risk, an organization called Asterisk Financial recently created a new product called Personal Guarantee Insurance™ (PGI). As stated on Asterisk Financial's website (www.personalguarantee.com), Personal Guarantee Insurance gives small and medium-sized business owners and commercial real estate investors protection for personal assets when they sign a personal guarantee for a commercial loan. If, after liquidating the business assets, the lender seeks personal assets to repay the balance of the loan, PGI will cover 30% to 70% of the insured's net liability, depending on the coverage purchased and the terms of the policy. [14]

As a former franchisee myself, I know just how nerve-racking signing a personal guarantee can be, so for those interested in reducing personal risk, this is worth checking out.

BASIC FUNCTION FOUR: FINANCIAL PLANNING

The best franchise finance people are not actually bean counters—as a matter of fact, they're the farthest thing from it. Good franchisors pay handsomely for top-notch financial experts who have the ability not only to "keep score" but to play an active role in virtually every aspect of the business. A good CFO, for example, will typically have a good understanding of the basic operations and marketing elements of the business and will not hesitate to share his or her insights and perspectives in these areas. In addition, a forwarding-thinking finance department will spend a good deal of their time working with the research and development department (or the CEO in the case of smaller franchisors), and evaluating new opportunities for growth. They will create detailed financial models and forecasts, and frequently play a critical role in presenting both the present- and future-growth picture to the board of directors or senior leadership of the company.

CHAPTER NOTES

CHAPTER 7: ELEMENT VI

13) "Franchise Financing Options" by Eddy Goldberg http://www.franchising.com/howtofranchiseguide/ franchise_financing_options.html

14) Asterisk Financial, Inc., 213 Court Street, Suite 610, Middletown, CT 06457, © 2012 Asterisk Financial, All rights reserved, http://www.personalguarantee.com/asterisk/ article/12/what-is-personal-guarantee-insurance

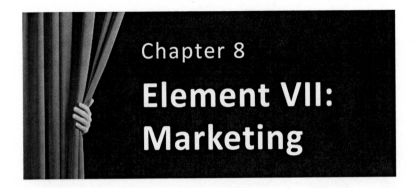

Chapter 8

Element VII: Marketing

One could easily write an entire book (or multiple books) regarding the art and science of franchise marketing, so if you're expecting a novel here, it's not going to happen. What I *am* providing, however, is an overview of the franchise marketing process from both the franchisee and franchisor perspective. Before we begin, let me say this: I like marketing people. I have found most marketing people to be fun, gregarious, and non-judgmental, and they tend to be very good at what they do.

ITEM 1: FRANCHISOR MARKETING

Marketing, from the franchisor perspective, is all about the acquisition of new franchisees. This, as you can imagine, is no easy feat (especially in these economically challenging times) and marketing people have had to become very innovative in their efforts to attract new blood. The marketing department (typically run by a vice president of marketing or a chief marketing officer [CMO]), works very closely with the franchise development department from both a strategic and tactical standpoint to create a comprehensive franchise development marketing plan. This plan typically includes the creation of multiple pieces of marketing collateral ("creative"), the delivery timing of the various elements ("cadence"), the specific types of media to be utilized ("channels"), and the marketing budget.

Franchise marketing these days is all about being in the right place at the right time with the right message (duh), but what makes franchise marketing unique is the need to leverage both the digital world *and* the physical world seamlessly, all while keeping the prospect on the hook through every stage. The most sophisticated franchisors have actually created automated online sales software, which guides the prospect through the qualification process via an interactive and visually stimulating stroll through the wonderful world of "X" franchise opportunity. These systems generally include video, audio, strategically placed pages requiring franchisee input, and an integrated (and automated) email system designed to gently remind the prospect that he or she needs to continue entering key information, or that he or she must return to the site to complete the candidate qualification process. As a technology junkie (read: nerd), I happen to think this is very cool, and I've personally been involved in the creation of a couple of these systems.

In addition, most franchisors will supplement their online marketing efforts with appearances at trade shows, advertisements in trade newspapers and magazines, and even good ol' direct mail.

A WARNING TO THE PROSPECTIVE FRANCHISEE:

Marketing materials are designed to be slick, beautiful, and enticing—that's the whole point. DO NOT be seduced by the pretty pictures of happy, perfect people having the time of their lives providing home health care or serving yogurt smoothies. Franchisors spend millions of dollars creating marketing materials designed to sell the dream of small-business ownership and the miracle that is "X" franchise opportunity. You...must...fight...the...urge...to...give...in. Look at the pretty pictures for a while, dream a few dreams, then put them away and start re-reading the FDD. If that doesn't bring you back to reality in a hurry, I don't know what will.

A WARNING

In several states, franchise marketing materials must actually be filed with the state's franchise regulatory agency, and beware of any materials that make financial performance representations that are inconsistent with the information provided in any Item 19 FPR's. If you ever see a marketing brochure or receive an email touting the piles of money you can make by becoming a franchisee, *run*. Then, report the company to the FTC or to the franchise regulators in your state, as this is a major franchising no-no.

ITEM 2: FRANCHISEE MARKETING

A franchisor who does not understand the fact that he or she *must* help his or her franchisees to generate sales is a franchisor who is not going be around very long. I've said it before and I'll say it again: A great franchisor focuses on the profitability of his or her *franchisees* first, and his or her profitability second (albeit a very close second). If franchisees aren't making money, they generally won't be happy no matter what else the franchisor has to offer, so helping franchisees to become (and remain) profitable is of paramount importance.

There are two general schools of thought when it comes to assisting franchisees with their marketing: the "Do It for Me" (DIFM) model and the "Do It Yourself" (DIY) model.

DIFM—Do It for Me franchisors generally have a strong desire to control their marketing messages and they are frequently very concerned about protecting their brand equity and trademarks. These franchisors tend to believe that their franchisees, as a whole, are not marketing experts, and are therefore not capable (or willing) to execute an effective marketing campaign on an ongoing basis. In addition, these types of franchisors like to maintain a high degree of control and they would much prefer to personally execute all marketing on behalf of their franchisees. DIFM franchisors tend to view their franchise marketing efforts as a profit center, and by essentially creating the equivalent of an ad agency, they can charge a service fee for their labors and pocket a percentage of the marketing dollars they collect. For franchisors who have a strong desire to maintain strict control of their messaging, this is not a bad way to go. In addition, franchisees may find this method attractive, in that they like the turnkey nature of the process so they can focus their energies on other elements of the business.

DIFM franchisors generally require their franchisees to contribute to a national ad fund, a local ad fund, or both. Some DIFM franchisors simply require their franchisees to contribute to a single general ad fund, which they then apportion between local, regional, and national marketing efforts. These types of franchisors usually do not require their franchisees to spend additional marketing and advertising dollars locally (beyond the amount they are contributing to the franchisor's general ad fund), although franchisees are typically permitted to do so *provided* the franchisor pre-approves the additional advertising expenditures.

DIFM franchisors typically utilize either a dedicated franchise marketing specialist or a franchise business consultant to provide the day-to-day tactical marketing support that a franchisee typically requires. This support can range from very basic support, such as answering general marketing questions regarding how and where to market, to more complex questions, such as how to create a strategic marketing plan. These tactical support roles are supported by a director or vice president of marketing, whose job it is to work with the president/CEO to create the overarching strategic marketing vision for the franchisor and to support the vision on a tactical basis at the local, regional, and national levels.

A NOTE FOR FRANCHISEES

A sophisticated franchisor's marketing department will often create a detailed strategic plan encompassing the various elements of the marketing process. This is sometimes referred to as a "strategy pyramid." At the top of the plan you'll find the franchisor's vision, followed by the mission, goals, strategies, tactics, and action plans. Don't be afraid to ask to see this plan when investigating a franchise concept. A franchisor who lacks this plan may be indicative of a general lack of operational organization, which is always a red flag.

Strategy Pyramid

DIY—Do It Yourself franchisors generally prefer to delegate the responsibility for marketing to their franchisees. For the most part, they believe that since their franchisees are more familiar with their own local markets than anyone else, they should be able to handle their own local marketing. While some of these DIY franchisors take a very hands-off stance relative to their franchisees (the franchisee is essentially responsible for everything from creative development to placement to vendor negotiations), most want to maintain some level of control. Enter the online ad-builder.

An ad-builder is essentially an online library of pre-approved marketing materials (creative) that can be accessed by the franchisee to create a multitude of different ads (direct mail, print, web-based, etc.). While ad-builders can run the gamut from very sophisticated to extremely simple, most systems will allow the franchisee to enter some basic information at the user-level (e.g., location name, address, phone number, etc.). Then, once the basic information has been entered, the franchisee can select from a menu of pre-approved offer templates, which will automatically merge the basic information into the ad, and *voila*—instant marketing collateral!

The beauty of these systems is that they not only greatly increase efficiency at the store level; they are basically idiot-proof. The most sophisticated systems will automatically forward a proof to the franchisor for final approval before allowing the franchisee to send out the completed ad copy, and some will even automatically deduct the cost of the ad from the franchisee's ad fund balance. Now that's slick!

Unlike DIFM franchisors, DIY franchisors generally require their franchisees to contribute to a national ad fund only, and these funds are spent for the benefit of all franchisees equally (versus regionally and/or locally). The marketing fund contribution for DIY franchisors is typically a lower percentage of gross revenue (versus a DIFM franchisor), because most DIY franchisors require their franchisees to spend a specified dollar amount or a percentage of gross revenues on local store advertising themselves, above and beyond their national ad fund contribution. Generally, most franchisors require their franchisees to prove that these local advertising dollars are being spent by requiring their franchisees to submit their paid advertising invoices to the franchisor on a regular basis. In some cases, a franchisor may agree to supplement (or match) franchisees' local advertising contributions. Some franchisors also may require a group of franchisees in a particular region to form a "marketing co-op" to pool their marketing dollars and fund more sophisticated marketing campaigns (e.g. television and radio advertising).

In a nutshell, DIY franchisors believe that their franchisees can be more successful by administering all local advertising themselves with limited operational support and guidance from the franchisor. DIY franchisors like the fact that they typically do not need to create the level of internal support processes that a DIFM must maintain to support their franchisees' marketing efforts.

A WARNING

Many franchisors have gotten themselves into trouble by not properly supervising their franchisees' marketing activities. Franchisees by their very nature are entrepreneurial beings, and when left unsupervised they can sometimes come up with some very...how should I put this..."creative" stuff. Many brands have been ruined by a franchisee who decided to add an unauthorized (read: inappropriate) graphic or offensive language to an ad, which subsequently ticked off the wrong people. Interestingly enough, many of these franchisees honestly believe that they are helping their brand, and truly have the best of intentions. This is frequently the case with regard to religious imagery or wording, which can be very offensive to some and cause significant damage to a brand (think: adding a Christian fish or Star of David symbol to an advertisement).

Regardless of the specific form of marketing support a franchisor provides (DIFM, DIY, or a combination of both), it is critical that all franchisors focus on driving inquiry volume to each of their franchise locations. There are three primary levels of marketing to which franchisors should devote their energies: national, regional, and local. Let's explore each of these in a bit more detail.

National Advertising: As mentioned earlier, almost all franchisors require their franchisees to contribute a portion of their gross revenue to a national marketing fund. All franchisees, regardless of the size of their operation(s), must contribute to the fund, which is then spent on marketing initiatives designed to benefit all franchisees. Although franchisees' contribution levels may vary, the fund is generalized in that the funds are spent on behalf of the franchise system as a whole. There is no guarantee that a franchisee will receive marketing in his or her region that is equivalent to the dollars that he or she contributed to the fund. Examples of national marketing/advertising activities include individual franchisee websites that are created for all franchisees based on a single template or "wire frame," television ads that can be customized locally (on a limited basis) but are designed to be used universally, and advertising collateral (such as direct mail) that can be customized locally (typically via an ad-builder) but that has universal applicability.

Regional Advertising: Few franchisors have a designated regional advertising fund that is separate from the national or local ad funds; however, some larger franchisors will contribute funds on a regional basis from either the national fund or, in some cases, the franchisor's general fund as a "co-op" (aka matching) contribution. Regional funds are typically allocated to a specific group of franchisees that comprise a region. Some regions are very large and can incorporate multiple states, while other regions, such as Orange County, California, are relatively small. The size of the region varies from franchise to franchise and is generally a function of the unit density in a given area.

Regional funds are often dedicated to support a specific group of franchisees who share a common marketing demographic or designated marketing area (DMA), and are used to increase exposure for all franchisees on a more localized basis. By banding together, groups of franchisees can often negotiate better buys for local advertising (particularly cable TV and/or public broadcasting), and they can work together as a group to increase their collective presence in a given market.

Ad Pools (aka Advertising Cooperatives): In some franchises (especially DIY models), franchisees are encouraged to band together regionally to form ad pools. An ad pool is a formalized marketing group, with elected officers, bylaws, and typically a local bank account. Franchisees get together on a regular basis (generally monthly, bi-monthly, or quarterly) to discuss regional marketing initiatives and to purchase advertising as a group. In this model, the franchisees agree on their regional advertising strategy and tactics, then typically deposit their funds into a joint account, which is then utilized to purchase marketing and advertising on behalf of the group. Although the franchisor always has the final say with regard to the advertising content, placement, and look/feel, the co-op usually has broad latitude with regard to how their collective advertising dollars are spent.

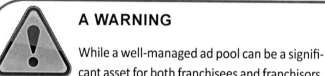

A WARNING

While a well-managed ad pool can be a significant asset for both franchisees and franchisors, a poorly managed ad pool can quickly become a nightmare. Franchisee conflicts and disagreements can and do arise for a multitude of reasons, and the resulting fallout can cause significant friction. When this occurs, the franchisor must frequently step in as a mediator, which is generally messy and complicated. In addition, the execution of national advertising initiatives, such as the implementation of individual franchisee websites for all locations, can be very difficult in an ad-pool-based system, as many ad pools will prefer to utilize their own online providers and systems. Unfortunately, many of these local providers will be of poor quality (think: my cousin Vinny or some other friend or buddy), which may harm both the local franchisees and the system as a whole.

Local Advertising: Of the three levels of advertising (national, regional, and local), local generally receives the lion's share of the attention, and in most franchise concepts, it is the most important. Although both national and regional advertising drive inquiries to a franchisee's location, even the largest franchisors frequently rely on local advertising to drive the majority of inquiry volume. Today, local store advertising plays an increasingly vital role in the success of many franchisees and franchisors, and the emphasis on local store advertising has increased dramatically in the past few years.

Local advertising typically includes a long list of advertising and marketing initiatives including (but not limited to) direct mail, coupon mailings (such as Valpak®), grass roots initiatives (such as sponsoring a little league team or handing out fliers at the local mall), ads in local newspapers and publications, and most importantly, web and mobile advertising. With regard to web-based local store advertising, an entire industry has sprung up to support this medium, and having a website specifically optimized for search engines, known as search engine optimization (SEO), with corresponding pay-per-click (PPC) and search engine marketing (SEM) elements, is no longer an option but a necessity. In addition, mobile (smartphone-based) marketing is becoming increasingly critical, and many franchisors are paying big bucks to create customized applications for the iPhone- and Android-based systems, in addition to new technologies such as geofencing, which allows individual franchisees to automatically send advertising to mobile phones within a specific radius of their facility.

A WORD TO THE WISE

A franchisor who is either unwilling or unable to invest in (or support) a comprehensive local online marketing program on behalf of his or her franchisees is a franchisor who just doesn't get it, and will most likely quickly fall behind. In this day and age, technology is not a "bonus" or a "frill"; it is a fundamental necessity that affects every franchisor and franchisee alike.

The Social Media Phenomenon: As of this writing, far too many franchisors still believe term "social media" is just another word for "smoke and mirrors," and most just don't understand the benefits of this powerful new medium. Although many franchisors are in the process of experimenting with social media to one degree or another, most would probably agree that if nothing else, websites such as Facebook and LinkedIn are an excellent means of increasing top-of-mind awareness and assessing the general pulse of a brand and how it's resonating in the real world. Increasingly, new forms of social marketing and advertising are extending the reach of the more traditional social media platforms, and the industry as a whole is evolving at light speed. Those that are willing and able to leverage these new tools are gaining a distinct competitive advantage, while those that refuse to evolve are (or will soon) pay the price. Don't believe me? Just take a look at the precipitous decline of traditional print media, or the staggering growth of Amazon and Apple. The future has arrived baby, and it's time to jump in with both feet!

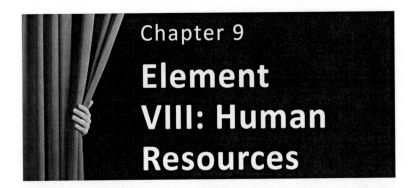

Chapter 9

Element VIII: Human Resources

The 35th president of the United States of America, John Fitzgerald Kennedy, once said, "The human mind is our fundamental resource." Love him or hate him (and seriously, how can you hate him?), JFK was one of the most influential figures in our political landscape, and he understood the need to leverage human capital. Whether you're a franchisor or a franchisee, hiring the right people at the right time for the right position will play a critical role in your future success.

The primary responsibility of the human resources department is to create, organize, and coordinate all of the elements related to the employees within the workplace. Primary responsibilities often include

- Hiring (recruiting, interviewing, negotiations, and contracts)

- Annual appraisals

- Employee benefits

- Training and continuing professional development

- Promotions and raises

- Warnings and layoffs

Many franchisors have become increasingly sophisticated when it comes to hiring their home office (aka "franchise support center") employees, and in assisting their franchisees with their own hiring needs. A significant percentage provide a broad range of support services such as sample job descriptions, interviewing tips and guidance, and assistance in obtaining reference and background checks. In the world of franchising, and in the business world in general, finding and retaining great people takes work and perseverance.

I've seen far too many franchisees and franchisors make the classic mistake of hiring the cheapest talent they can find, and some have even told me, with pride, that if they can find someone who can "fog a mirror," they'll hire them. *Yikes*! Of course, these are the same franchisees and franchisors who also tend to have *major* employee retention issues (not to mention inventory shrinkage and sexual harassment complaints), but hey, at least their labor is "cheap," right?

On the other hand, I've also had the good fortune of working with a number of franchisors and franchisees who really take pride in their hiring practices. As a matter of fact, the majority of franchisors and franchisees that I've either worked for or with were always very good about hiring slowly and firing quickly, which is one of the golden rules of HR. In an ironic twist, I've found that, from a franchisor perspective, many spend significantly more time vetting their support center employees than they do their franchisees. Hmmm. I wonder what that says about their priorities?

So, how does one go about finding great talent? Well, in my days as a franchisee I found the following techniques to be very successful:

1) Pay attention when you interact with someone who provides exceptional service. Does he smile when he talks?

Does she maintain eye contact? Can he put together a complete sentence without saying, "um," "like," or "you know" a dozen times? Does she make you feel like buying? Can he actually *sell* versus just taking an order? If you answered yes to most of these questions, you may just be looking at your next employee. I always kept a pocketful of my business cards when I went out, and every time I encountered someone who provided outstanding service, or who demonstrated a number of the traits listed above, I'd hand him or her my business card and say, "You have a terrific personality, and I can tell that you're very good at what you do. If you're ever interested in working for a great organization where you'll be treated with respect and have a real career path, please give me a call." I almost always received a call within two weeks, and my employees were second to none (if I do say so myself).

A WORD TO THE WISE

Restaurants and retail stores are frequently great sources of quality personnel leads if you're in the market for customer-facing service people.

2) If you're using a job board such as Monster.com or Careerbuilder.com, write a great add and customize it with your company logo, etc. Be sure to include a bit of background about your organization, and for goodness' sake, proofread your material!

3) Ask for references from friends, colleagues, and family. Some of my best hires came from personal references, and nothing has more credibility than a reference from a trusted source.

So now that you have your new employee on board, how do you ensure that he or she will delight your customers and provide consistent and superior service excellence? Please read on.

HR AND TRAINING

For franchisees and franchisors alike, it's all about managing the customer experience, and training employees in the ways to deliver it—in every transaction, every day. Put simply, the success of your franchise operation is directly proportional to the quality of your employees' behaviors and attitudes. So how do you ensure that your employees are truly a reflection of the image you want to portray? Why, training, of course!

Training any new employee always begins with the initial employment interview. Taking the time to screen and interview new employees is crucial. The problem for many small-business owners (and franchisors, for that matter), is that companies always seem to need their new employees yesterday. Balancing the urgency of filling a position with finding high-quality employees is an ongoing challenge, but skimping on or rushing the hiring process is *not* the answer. It's been said that skills can be taught, but attitude is something that has to come from within. While I've occasionally encountered individuals with a great attitude who were thick as mud, for the most part I would agree with this statement.

A NOTE FOR FRANCHISEES

Hiring can be a tricky skill set. As an employer you must not only be adept at judging character; you must also comply with a long list of laws and regulations if you want to stay out of court. If you're not familiar with exactly what you can and cannot say during the hiring process, *do not* just wing it. Consult your franchisor's HR department or your operations manual, or, if you're really in need of some help, you may want to consider hiring a third party to help you screen candidates. Following is a brief list of questions that can get you into hot water quickly during the interview process:

- Are you married?
- Do you have children?
- How old are you?
- Do you plan to get pregnant?
- Do you have a disability or chronic illness?
- Where were you born?
- Do you observe Yom Kippur?
- Are you in the National Guard?
- What is your native language?
- Do you smoke or use alcohol?

AN IMPORTANT NOTE FOR FRANCHISORS

Although assisting franchisees with basic resource-related training is a fundamental value-added service that all franchisors should provide, it's important to note that a franchisee's employees are *not* employees of the franchisor. In fact, employee relations between a franchisee and his or her employees can actually be quite a headache for a franchisor, because of a concept called vicarious liability. Essentially, if a franchisor overreaches and actively controls the employee relationship between the franchisee and his or her employee, then the franchisor may be liable under the legal theory of vicarious liability.

One way for franchisors to minimize this vicarious liability challenge is to insist that *all* materials provided to franchisee employees—employee handbooks, code of conduct documents, contracts, etc.—be franchisee-specific and separate and distinct from any materials provided by the franchisor. In addition, a franchisor may restrict any company-provided training (such as regional training classes) to a franchisee's designated in-house training representative, as opposed to training *all* of the franchisee's staff members. That way, the franchisor can say he or she was essentially training the trainer versus training all employees directly.

The bottom line when it comes to franchisee staffing and human resource needs, is that a good franchisor will offer the training and staff necessary to support the franchisee's hiring needs, while still maintaining an arms-length relationship. A franchisor who provides little or no assistance or guidance is simply not putting the franchisee's needs first, and that's always a red flag.

A DOUBLE WARNING FOR FRANCHISEES *AND* FRANCHISORS

Based on my personal experience, I cannot overemphasize the importance of conducting background checks for EVERY employee.

In one of my previous lives, while working in an operations support role in the children's entertainment arena, I would occasionally assist franchisees with the employment screening process. Although the vast majority of applicants appeared to be fine, upstanding citizens, occasionally I'd come across some real doozies. Like the convicted pedophile who was particularly interested in leading birthday parties (shocker), or the accountant who had embezzled a bunch of cash at her former company just a few months prior to applying for a senior accountant role. I know that money is tight (especially for new franchises); however, the few bucks you "save" by not properly screening your employees can and will bite you in the butt down the road.

A Very Brief Summary of I-9 and E-Verify

As if the interview and background check processes aren't complicated enough, all employers are required by law to employ only individuals who may legally work in the U.S.—either U.S. citizens or foreign citizens who have the necessary authorization. When discussing employment eligibility, the two most common topics that will generally arise are the I-9 employment eligibility verification document and the relatively new E-Verify program, launched in 1997 as a pilot program. E-Verify is closely linked to Form I-9, and exists to strengthen the Form I-9 employment eligibility verification process that all employers, by law, must follow. While participation in E-Verify is voluntary for most employers, completion of Form I-9 is required of all employers. If you're interested in learning more about this program, please visit www.uscis.gov/everify—or better yet, hire a competent HR person who knows the score.

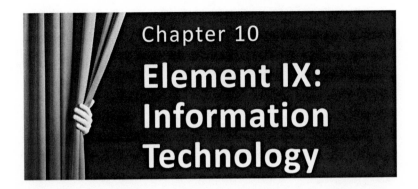

Chapter 10

Element IX: Information Technology

W e live in a wired (or wireless) age, and as businesses have become increasingly sophisticated, many franchisors have invested heavily in technology and systems infrastructure. As franchising is essentially the management of many small independently owned businesses operating in harmony, technology has evolved to provide franchisors with an unprecedented level of control and business intelligence (BI) at an enterprise level.

Many franchisors have developed digital "dashboards" that provide critical information based on a hierarchy of needs (manager, director, VP, etc.). These dashboards generally provide key performance indicator (KPI) data that is constantly monitored at the store level and either pushed out to the franchisor automatically or pulled in by the franchisor on an as-needed basis. In addition, many franchisors have created or purchased sophisticated intranet systems that allow the franchisor to store critical information such as operations manuals and communication archives, and additionally, allow for the instant communication of vital information to the entire network with just a few keystrokes.

The most sophisticated systems have evolved from basic websites to all-inclusive franchise portals designed to be a one-stop-shop for both franchisees and franchisors. This portal design essentially requires the franchisee to access the portal on a daily basis, as this is where all of the critical communications and business operational data are stored. In other words, accessing the portal becomes as essential and routine as opening the front door, and franchisors who have adopted this type of system have improved their franchisee communication effectiveness dramatically.

A NOTE FOR FRANCHISORS

Investing in a robust digital infrastructure has quickly evolved from a luxury to a necessity. Many quality franchise-specific software companies provide a robust, multi-tiered platform designed to address virtually every aspect of franchise management. Typical features include

- franchise development
- franchise performance and royalty management
- franchise relationship, collaboration, and training
- franchise operations
- franchise marketing
- franchise e-commerce and point-of-sale

A NOTE FOR FRANCHISEES

It's been said that it takes approximately 28 days of consecutive repetition to establish a habit. In the franchising world, many franchisors have figured out that one of the primary keys to franchisee success is to establish the right habits as quickly as possible, which is why successful franchisors tend to be sticklers for doing things "their way." From a technological standpoint, this means ensuring that all franchisees are operating in the same (or very similar) manner on a daily basis, which is why the most successful franchisors require their franchisees to log into an intranet every day. It's a generally accepted fact that after approximately one month of accessing a company's intranet on a daily basis, a franchisee will continue to do so for as long as he or she remains with the organization. And these days, a franchisee can log in remotely from virtually anywhere in the world. Many franchisors have even moved to a mobile platform whereby franchisees and franchisors have instant access to their key performance data right from their smartphones! This is one of the key elements driving the growth of multi-unit ownership for many concepts.

I have personally used both the FranConnect©[15] and IFX©[16] products, two of the most recognized and popular franchise management systems in the industry, and both are remarkably robust. I can recall one instance where I was attempting to train a group of more tenured franchisees on how to utilize a new intranet reporting portal. These "seasoned" franchisees had been among the first group to sign on with the franchisor (well before the advent of the digital age), and they were very set in their ways, to say the least. Add to this the fact that the franchisor had done a poor job of communicating with the franchise community in general, and had been slow to provide any valid performance measurement data, and I had one volatile mixture on my hands.

Once the initial rollout and training was complete, most of the franchisees were at least willing to give the new system a shot, so for the next 30 days all of the franchise business consultants were mobilized to provide one-on-one coaching with every franchisee on a daily basis to ensure that our "no franchisee left behind" initiative was successful (original, I know). At the end of the 30-day period, 90% of the franchisees were utilizing the new portal on a daily basis, and at the 60-day mark we achieved the magical 100% utilization rate.

A WORD TO THE WISE FOR FRANCHISORS

The moral of the story: There are a lot of ways to screw up a franchise, and one of the classics is to communicate poorly and provide substandard business management tools. While the adoption of new technology is commendable, doing so without a well-crafted implementation plan is tantamount to planning a vacation without an itinerary. It takes a *tremendous* amount of effort to launch a new initiative in a franchise system, and when in doubt, it's best to err on the side of over-communication and assistance.

CHAPTER NOTES

CHAPTER 10: ELEMENT IX

15) Copyright © 2004-2012 FranConnect, Inc. All rights reserved. www.franconnect.com

16) Copyright © 2010 IFX International, Inc. All Rights Reserved. www.ifxonline.com

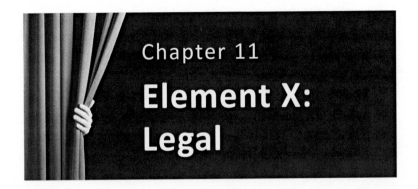

I have been a member of the International Franchise Association (IFA) for many years, and every time I attend a conference or convention I am amazed by the staggering number of franchise attorneys in attendance. It frequently feels like a 1:1 ratio of attendees to attorneys, and I'll tell you this: The attorneys aren't there because they have nothing better to do. Franchising is a highly regulated industry, and given the unique relationship between franchisees and franchisors, there is no shortage of potential sources of conflict. Greedy franchisors and franchisees can—and do—make some stupid and selfish decisions that often result in legal actions. While many books have been written on this subject, the purpose of *this* book is to provide a look behind the franchise curtain, so let's take a peek at a few of the ways in which the legal community is involved in the world of franchising from both a franchisor and franchisee perspective.

FRANCHISOR LEGAL SUPPORT: Most larger franchisors have full-time in-house legal departments devoted entirely to providing legal support. Those franchisors who do not have the scale to support in-house counsel typically have an attorney, or multiple attorneys, on speed dial. Why, you ask, is legal support such an integral component of franchising? The answer has to do with the FTC and the need to be extremely cautious right out of the gate when the decision is first made to become a franchisor.

Remember the first element of this book—the FDD and the franchise agreement? Who do you think typically creates and reviews the FDD and the franchise agreement? You guessed it: an attorney. So right from the start, attorneys are involved in the initial setup of the franchise framework, and they quickly position themselves as a trusted and indispensable resource. Now, I am not anti-attorney by any means, and as a matter of fact, I have had the good fortune of working with many competent and professional attorneys over the years and have found them to be an indispensable asset. That being said, I have also worked with attorneys whose entire goal in life is to find disgruntled franchisees and "help" them to understand that what they *really* need to do is sue their franchisor to get ahead. Let's take a closer look at the world of the franchise attorney.

For many franchisees and franchisors, their introduction to the world of franchising law begins with the need to create and/or review the FDD and the franchise agreement. One of the first significant investments a new franchisor makes is the creation of the FDD and the filing/registration of this document in a number of states across the country. Not all states require filing/registration, and some states' requirements are more stringent than others; however, if a franchisor intends to sell his or her concept in any state, a franchising attorney should be consulted to ensure full compliance with the law. As detailed in Element I of this book, franchising is a heavily regulated industry, and seeking out quality legal advice and support is the best way to stay out of trouble.

From the franchisee standpoint, it is always wise to find a good franchising attorney, as there are several key times during the franchise ownership lifecycle where a good attorney will prove invaluable:

1) **During the initial due diligence phase:** When considering any franchise, a franchising attorney can provide some excellent insights into the quality and overall "health" of the organization.

2) **During the normal course of operations:** Situations *will* arise where the franchise agreement must be consulted, and a competent attorney can help to interpret and explain the nuances of the agreement.

3) **If things get ugly and a dispute arises (which is unfortunately not uncommon in franchising):** An attorney will play a critical role in addressing (and hopefully resolving) the dispute.

For franchisors, having good legal counsel on board (or on call) is not a luxury; it's a necessity, and an expense that MUST be included in any budget. Attorneys are involved in many elements of the franchising process, including the following (just to name a few):

1) Preparing and filing the initial FDD and registering trademarks with the United States Patent and Trademark Office

2) Assisting with franchise sales compliance training and documentation

3) The review of all franchise sales materials, both in hardcopy and digital formats

4) Counsel and guidance relating to the signing of each franchise agreement and the vetting of all new franchisees

5) Handling relationship issues with franchisees

In summary, it's safe to say that whether you're a franchisor or franchisee, having a great franchise attorney on your team is one of the most vital ingredients for success.

AN IMPORTANT NOTE

Keep in mind that just because a law firm is big, it does not mean it's the best. While some people prefer to deal with a large, well-known firm, other people find that smaller firms offer more personalized service and/or more reasonable rates. Bottom line here: Do your homework and be sure to interview a minimum of three firms. And don't be shy about asking potential franchise attorneys about what differentiates them from other law firms—they should have that answer down pat.

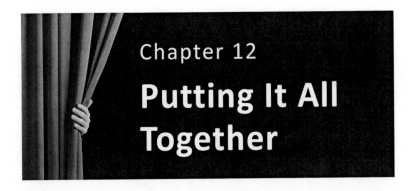

Chapter 12

Putting It All Together

And there you have it—a look behind the franchise curtain from a uniquely straightforward, no-B.S. perspective. The Ten Key Elements of Franchising, as outlined, represent the heart and soul of every franchising organization regardless of its size, product, or location.

For high-functioning franchisors and franchisees, most of these elements will be green on an ongoing basis, and on a few rare occasions, all of the elements just may be green simultaneously. The key to building a viable, healthy, and productive franchise is to *continuously* track each of the Ten Elements while focusing on achieving and maintaining a green status across the board. As with most endeavors in life, this is much easier said than done.

While franchising can be an incredibly powerful business format, for many uninitiated franchisees and franchisors the concept can at first blush appear deceptively simple. Do not be fooled. For a franchise to flourish, ALL parties must "win," which requires everyone to do the right thing…all the time. Greed and self-interest have killed many a dream for both franchisors and franchisee alike, and if you can't look at yourself in the mirror every night and truly say that you've done what's right, you probably haven't. Great franchising is about telling it like it is, doing what's right, and working hard to achieve your dream. So now that you know what *really* goes on behind the franchise curtain, **Be Good To Each Other**™, get out there, and WIN!

To learn more, please visit www.goodfran.com.

About the Author

As the son of a Stanford professor, Richard J. "Rick" Basch grew up in an environment where education and hard work were prized above all else. Over the course of his nearly two-decades-long career in franchising, Rick has become an accomplished franchise consultant whose unique industry perspective is rooted in his broad base of personal experiences. As both a former franchisee *and* a senior franchising executive, Rick has truly seen both sides of the coin.

From his early beginnings as a single-unit franchisee, Rick learned exactly what it takes to survive as a small-business owner, and it was his time in the trenches that defined and shaped his "we need to win together" perspective. After a successful stint as a franchisee, Rick was invited by his then franchisor to join the corporate organization, first as a franchise business consultant, then as the director of company-owned stores, and finally as the vice president of franchise operations. In subsequent years, Rick has worked for a number of franchisors in various executive roles, including vice present and president, representing a broad spectrum of concepts ranging in size from as few as 50 employees to as many as 200,000.

Rick's lifelong love of learning and education and his thirst for knowledge can be summed up in the "alphabet soup" after his name—MBA, CFE (certified franchise executive), PMP (project management professional), and a host of others. A self-proclaimed "franchise junkie," Rick's fondest wish is to build world-class franchising organizations and to share with the world what really goes on *Behind the Franchise Curtain.* In his current role as founder and CEO of GoodFran Franchise Consulting, LLC, Rick is living his dream of providing high-quality franchise consulting services to both current and prospective franchisors and franchisees, and his slogan, **Be Good To Each Other**™, is a call to action for the franchising industry.

To learn more, please visit www.goodfran.com.

Index

Index

CPSIA information can be obtained at www.ICGtesting.com
Printed in the USA
LVOW081408220712

290738LV00005B/24/P